NEW FRONTIERS IN GOLD

THE DERIVATIVES REVOLUTION

JESSICA CROSS

ROSENDALE PRESS

Copyright © 1994 Jessica Cross

Illustrations © 1994 Dr Rob

First published in Great Britain in 1994 by
Rosendale Press Ltd
Premier House
10 Greycoat Place
London SW1P 1SB

Jacket and book design by Pep Reiff
Cartoons by Dr Rob
Production: Edward Allhusen, Old House Books

ISBN 1 872803 18 0

Typesetting: Ace Filmsetting Ltd, Frome, Somerset

Printed in the United Kingdom by the Cromwell Press

British Library Cataloguing in Publication Data
A catalogue record for this book is available from The British Library.

CONTENTS

PREFACE

This book attempts to answer the many questions surrounding a group of sophisticated paper-based commercial products collectively termed derivatives, the emergence of which has heralded an irrevocable transformation of the commodity and financial markets. I have concentrated on the gold market because that is where much of my experience lies, but I have yet to meet a market that remains unaffected by what can only be termed the derivatives revolution.

I first became fully aware of the derivative markets in January 1988 as I stood alongside the gold futures and options pits on the Commodity Exchange floor in New York. Being a novice, I thought that 'the pit' seemed a fitting term for what I observed to be a seething mass of men swarming around in faded blue or orange jackets, shouting incoherently and frantically waving their arms in what appeared to be a rather pointless exercise. I realised how little I knew about the world of derivatives. In fact, I was so ignorant about the paper markets that I did not even know what questions to ask to find out what I needed to know.

I was soon to appreciate that the late 1980s and early 1990s saw the meteoric emergence of financial derivatives in most commodities, and developments in the gold market were no exception. Global liberalisation of markets, 24 hour trading and very sophisticated computer software all played their role.

While most financial and commodity markets were already using derivatives on a daily basis, in many cases in a way that was second nature to the participants, I found huge voids in the literature associated with the various products, especially as regards gold. Volumes had already been written about the Black and Scholes model and option pricing, but these daunting books were peppered liberally with mathematical equations and complex jargon, which I had difficulty understanding.

This was not what I was looking for. I was after a clear, concise and, most importantly, an understandable explanation of delta hedging. I was looking for estimates of total outstanding gold forward positions, OTC options and gold loans on a year-end basis in order to assess averaged weighted achieved prices. I wanted to understand the rationale behind producer hedging which I knew had to be more than 'secure the contango'. I wanted to see, set out logically and calmly, the pros and cons of hedging. I needed to decide for myself whether producer hedging was a good thing. Above all, I wanted to understand how this flurry of apparently unrelated paper activity influenced the price of gold in the short, medium and long term. That is what this book is about.

In a sense, this book is also an exercise in communication. The derivative market tends to be shrouded in jargon accessible only to those who either create and market the products or those who make regular use of them. Newcomers are confronted by a bewildering and totally unnecessary language barrier which only serves to delay their entry into what otherwise could be a very available and potentially lucrative market. My aim therefore in writing this book is to breach the communications barrier between the creator of the derivative and the customer. Therefore I have made a conscious effort to avoid lapsing into derivative jargon. Where derivative-related terms are used and appear in **bold**, a full definition can be found in the glossary of terms.

As a commodity analyst, I was lucky to find exactly the right research field at precisely the right time. In January 1988 I was working on the Consolidated Gold Fields Annual Gold Survey. That provided me with the time and platform to monitor the derivatives revolution. The market itself and my interest in it developed simultaneously.

Researching what essentially is a virtually invisible market was not easy and it required a grass roots approach. What saved the day was a pool of immensely knowledgeable gold market participants, the vast majority of whom were kind enough to invest their valuable time in me and were willing to share insights into their particular area of expertise. Without them, I would have had virtually nothing to show for my efforts and I will always be extremely grateful to the collective gold market, many of whom have become close friends.

I am deeply indebted to every mining company treasurer and bullion dealer who took the time to reply to my surveys which gave invaluable insights into the overall structure of the derivatives markets. I would particularly like to thank Professor David Potts of the Department of Mineral Resources Engineering at Nottingham University, and Timothy Green of Rosendale Press, himself a writer and consultant on gold, for recognising very early on the need to assess paper markets and for their kindness and support throughout my years of work. Andy Smith of UBS and Ted Arnold of Merrill Lynch were always there in London on the other end of a telephone and they listened, albeit sometimes bemusedly.

Finally, my thanks to James, my husband and companion, who proved to be the one man who could answer my questions, especially when they were not about the gold market.

Jessica Cross
London, Johannesburg, 1994

1

WHAT ARE DERIVATIVES?

After many years of researching and writing about derivatives, including a doctoral thesis, I suddenly realised that I have never publicly defined what is meant by the term derivative. Scanning the literature, I have found that I am by no means the exception but rather the rule. It is as though gold market participants intuitively know what derivatives are, but we appear to shy away from defining them, certainly in any general sense.

One of the best definitions that I have come across appeared in the Group of 30 report, *Derivatives: Practices and Principles*, which explains that a derivative is: 'a bi-lateral contract . . . whose value derives . . . from the value of an underlying asset or underlying reference rate or index'[1].

While this certainly covers derivatives as financial products primarily for investment purposes, it does not adequately cover some of the financial mechanisms which I have historically considered a derivative of some sort. This definition, for example, does not cover the gold loan, which is a means of raising capital, the success of which is based on the gold price at the time of draw down, relative to any subsequent price performance. Certainly as far as gold is concerned I would, therefore,

---

[1] *Derivatives: Practices and Principles*, Group of 30, Washington, 1993, p28

expand the definition to include any predominantly paper product, usually highly leveraged, whose value, but also its usefulness to its owner and the very purpose for its existence, is directly or indirectly dependent on the price of physical gold. In other words, the gold price is ultimately the basic point of reference from which the success or failure of any bullion derivative is judged.

This book, therefore, includes the **exchange based futures and options**, the forward market, the **over-the-counter (OTC)** options, **gold-backed bonds** and **gold loans**. While some may argue that gold loans are not strictly derivatives, it would be inappropriate not to deal with them, especially after their contribution to the supply side of the gold market throughout the mid and late 1980s.

WHY DERIVATIVES: WHAT IS SO SPECIAL ABOUT THEM?

Unlike other market sectors, derivatives are relatively new to gold. While exchange futures and options have been traded since 1972, it is essentially only in the last decade that the gold business has been subject to the whole host of derivatives in sufficient volume to influence the market and consequently the metal's price. All other commodities and financial products are now subject to derivative activity in some form or other and in varying degrees. The only differences have been in timing and the manner in which each market has responded to the onset of the derivative revolution.

The word revolution really is the only way to describe adequately what has happened. As the Group of 30 report says, 'The creation and widespread use of global derivatives in the past 15 years have changed the face of finance'[2]. The currencies and financials were the first to see the emergence of derivatives. Precious metals (with the possible exception of the platinum group metals, primarily because of long-term contracts between producers and consumers) followed shortly afterwards. This was probably because of gold's and, to a lesser degree, silver's residual monetary characteristics. The base metals, mainly copper, nickel and aluminum, are now also getting their fair share of derivative buffeting.

My intention in this book is to review how derivatives have swiftly

[2] Ibid

An Option and its Derivatives

become an integral part of the gold market and how this has irrevocably altered the nature of the bullion business. It is not the intention to expose readers to incomprehensible option jargon and daunting mathematical formulae – quite the contrary, I have gone to lengths to avoid this. The aim is to answer the question: what do derivatives mean for me and my business? The corporate 'me' might refer to refiners, miners, jewellery fabricators, central bankers, bullion dealers and investors.

I do not claim to have all the answers. In many instances we simply do not know yet about the suitability of specific products or we do not have a sufficiently long enough data series to draw any definitive conclusions. I take comfort from the fact that the market is asking the right questions, that the subject of derivatives now appears regularly on most gold conference programmes and that they are openly being discussed by all concerned.

My definition of derivatives carefully included the phrase 'highly leveraged'. I believe that this phrase, or sometimes 'highly geared', is the key to understanding how the derivatives have imposed their presence on the rest of the gold market. Gearing has become synonymous with derivatives, especially options, and of course not just in gold. Option leverage represents possibly one of the products' greatest assets but also one of their most serious liabilities.

The **premium** paid for an option is always only a small proportion of the total value of its underlying commodity so, with little in the way of capital outlay, buyers of gold options can acquire a relatively large potential exposure to gold. A simple hypothetical example demonstrates this. An investor who, in the hope of a rising price, buys one ounce of gold, at say $400 per ounce, has to immediately lay out 100 percent of the value of the investment. But if that investor was to buy a **call option** which would give the right to buy gold at say $430, the investor would only be required to pay for the cost of the option, say a hypothetical $4 per ounce. This implies that the investor, for the same capital outlay as for one ounce of gold, can take a potential **long** position of 100 ounces. This is all that is meant when the market talks about gearing.

If the potential benefit of dealing in options can be in excess of 100 times greater than that of dealing in the physical metal, then the potential risk of the exposure is equally great, should the gold price move against the writer of an option. This is why I maintain that the highly leveraged nature is both the beauty and the beast within the derivative. Like the little girl in the nursery rhyme, when derivatives are good they are very very good, but when they are bad they are horrid. It all depends on how they are used.

Like a drug correctly prescribed and used, a derivative can transform, strengthen and heal an ailing balance sheet. But abuse that drug, unwittingly or otherwise, and it can turn on the corporate body or entity, undermining its overall well being. Ultimately, because of the derivative's gearing, this could bring a company to its knees. We have already seen some spectacular defaults and losses associated with derivative products. Metallgesellschaft, Proctor & Gamble and Koshima Oil may not be directly involved with gold derivatives but these skeletons are going to keep rattling out of treasury cupboards for many years to come.

Some market participants say it will not happen in gold. I remember the very first time I spoke about the potential influence that the derivatives could have on gold, at the Financial Mail Conference in Johannesburg in 1990. The audience, mostly miners, was incredulous with disbelief: this will not happen in gold – gold is different. I got the same response in London, two years later, when I alerted the base metal markets to what had already happened in gold. Gold is different, they said, this will not happen in base metals. It has.

Commodities may be different but they are all being subjected to virtually the same derivatives. The rate of growth in derivatives and their degree of leverage has now caused a great deal of concern about their possible effect on financial markets in general. This concern is only being exacerbated by a spate of onerous defaults and company failures, many of which have been blamed on derivatives. However, it is arguable whether the products themselves are to blame or whether the fault lies with the manner in which they have been applied. Thus the issue of regulation of derivatives is, and will continue to be, a lively debate to which I add my own thoughts in the final chapter of this book.

2

WHAT CAN THE
EXCHANGES OFFER?

I once compared derivatives to a bill of fare[1]. The principal-to-principal, or over-the-counter, derivative products became the *à la carte* menu, dishes individually ordered to suit the customer. The exchange futures and options contracts, being standard products, appeared on the set menu. Today, the gastronomic analogy is more apt than ever with the set menu unchanged but the *à la carte* menu becoming increasingly rich and exotic in order to tempt discerning diners.

FIRST STEPS IN FUTURES

The first of January 1975 was an auspicious day for the gold market – the day the owning of gold by private citizens of the United States became legal. As a direct result, in January 1975, five commodity exchanges began offering and trading gold futures contracts[2]. Two of these were in New York, namely the Commodity Exchange (COMEX) and the New York Mercantile Exchange (NYMEX). The other three were located in

---

[1] Jacks , Jessica, 'The Importance of Hedging and Gold Loans in Mining Finance', paper presented at the Financial Times World Gold Conference, Vienna, 24 June 1991
[2] *Gold 1980* , Consolidated Gold Fields Gold Survey, London, 1981

Chicago – the International Monetary Market (IMM), the Mid America Exchange and the Chicago Board of Trade (CBOT).

However, the Big Apple and the Windy City cannot take the credit for being the first, since the legislation applicable to the USA did not apply to Canada. Two contracts (400oz and 100oz) were offered by the Winnipeg Commodity Exchange in 1972[3]. These two contracts never really managed to establish themselves and the three year trading volume, just prior to the liberalisation of the USA markets, totalled a meagre 116,229 contracts[4]. Liquidity and volume of turnover is paramount to the survival of a futures contract, and consequently the emergence and rapid acceptance of the COMEX contract, with its emphasis in the international financial centre of New York, initially attracted business away from Winnipeg[5] and later from Chicago[6]. In reality, COMEX became the futures market for gold, save TOCOM in Tokyo, which is more focused on Japanese business.

As with any derivative, there were initial reservations about the methodology and usefulness to the gold and financial community in general of these contracts. These included worries that the futures exchanges would attract money that would otherwise go into productive investment; that the futures markets were highly speculative; that the exchanges were subject to too many controls and too much required disclosure; and that the physical gold stocks held in the United States were insufficient to cover the trading volumes. Two decades later, the exchange futures have undergone some rationalisation, but the contract is an integral part of the gold market, without which many participants would have difficulty operating.

The contract specifications remain virtually unchanged and, as I will demonstrate, this is in stark contrast to the **principal-to-principal** forward market where product development has been nothing short of awesome.

THE BASIC FUTURES CONTRACT

The exchanges offer a public standard futures contract which provides

---

[3] Green, Timothy, *The New World of Gold*, revised edition, George Weidenfield & Nicholson Ltd, London, 1985
[4] *Gold 1980*, Consolidated Gold Fields Gold Survey, London, 1981
[5] Green, Timothy, *The New World of Gold*
[6] *Gold 1988*, Consolidated Gold Fields Gold Survey, London, 1989

fabricators, producers, speculators and investors with a means of minimising price risk and maximising profit potential. The exchanges are essentially administrative bodies which do not take a position in the market, but merely provide participants with the facilities to lock in specific prices for bullion due for future delivery (and of course, options, which I discuss shortly).

The exchanges are, therefore, non-profit and self-governing organisations operating under a set of regulations adhered to by all traders. Exchange membership is limited and is purchased and renewed annually after the board of directors has satisfied itself about the applicant's financial, commercial and moral status[7].

In the mid-1990s, COMEX was essentially the cornerstone gold trading exchange. However, COMEX itself merged with the New York Mercantile Exchange (NYMEX) in 1994, to become a self-governing subsidiary of the latter. But in most gold traders' minds COMEX is still *the* marketplace. So, despite the marriage, I use COMEX as my designation. The exchange, like the other nine US exchanges trading commodities, is regulated by the Commody Futures Trading Commission (CFTC). The CFTC is an independent government agency, established in 1975, to administer the provisions under the Commodity Exchange Act which places all exchange related commodity trading (futures and options) under federal jurisdiction. Each exchange has a clearing house which is responsible for co-ordinating daily transactions. This means that the exchange acts as a middleman and, unlike the over-the-counter (OTC) derivative market, there is no contact between the buyer and the seller. If you buy an exchange futures contract you never know the identity of the seller.

HOW DOES THIS WORK?

The COMEX futures contract is for 100oz of 995 fine gold for delivery in any one of six months: February, April, June, August, October and December. Contracts can be arranged for delivery in those set months up to five years ahead to allow producers long-term hedges. On a day-to-day basis, orders to buy and sell are placed and channelled from the dealing member through to the gold pit where they are executed by open outcry. Confirmation of the transaction is then reported back to the dealing firm

[7] *Gold 1980*, Consolidated Gold Fields Gold Survey, London, 1981

where the time of the transaction is recorded and the transaction is sent to the clearing house.

Each futures contract has a buyer and a seller. All transactions each day must be matched, processed and offset against each other and with the members before dealing can begin the following day. As a member dealer enters into a transaction on behalf of a client, a margin is payable of between 5–20% depending on the client's credit rating. This stands as a deposit or security against any adverse movement in the price. Since the margin is only a small proportion of the total value of the underlying metal, the futures contract is substantially more leveraged than a spot transaction. The margin is, in a way, similar to an option **premium**, although it continues throughout the life of a futures contract and if the price moves against the investor it is necessary to post additional margin, which can prove onerous. In contrast, an option premium is a one-off payment when the deal is executed.

The exchange clearing system and the CFTC has normally coped well, given the volume of business that can be completed in a short space of time. However, on occasions the strain has proved too great. A real test occurred in April 1987, initially in response to a sharp movement in the silver price. As the silver pit on the COMEX floor was adjacent to the gold pit and excitement and activity in one pit tends to spread to surrounding pits, the turnover of gold futures traded that April soared. The exchange then experienced one of its busiest months in its history, with over 54,000 contracts compared to 28,000 the previous month, and the clearing system simply could not cope with the paper work. COMEX was forced to close briefly as the clearing house staff tried to clear literally thousands of unmatched transactions[8].

Even after this period of administrative reconciliation, the clearing house was left with numerous unmatched contracts and it became apparent that some member dealers had conveniently 'lost' loss-making transactions. COMEX was severely criticised by the CFTC and the exchange's clearing procedures came under close scrutiny. Four member dealers were each fined $25,000 for unmatched dealings and a number of structural changes were made to the clearing mechanism, including the removal of a $25 per day limit in either direction on price movements.

This spate of business in 1987 shows up on the following table of gold futures volume, which also illustrates COMEX's unique position. Gold

[8] *Gold 1988*, Consolidated Gold Fields Gold Survey, London, 1989

futures on other US exchanges virtually faded out by 1991. In Tokyo, TOCOM turnover has grown substantially and that exchange has eased its rules to permit more foreign participation. On the international scene, however, COMEX remains the magnet.

Gold Futures Contract Volume
Annually 1985–1993

Thousands

	1985	1986	1987	1988	1989	1990	1991	1992	1993
US Exchanges									
COMEX (100oz)	7,774	8,400	10,240	9,496	9,989	9,730	6,800	5,002	8,916
TOCOM Tokyo (1kg)	548	1,030	2,159	2,038	2,687	6,873	4,568	4,194	3,764
CME/IMM (100oz)	0	0	262	0	0	0	0	0	0
CBOT (1kg)	169	125	160	103	28	37	18		
CBOT (100oz)	0	0	25	85	73	8	1		
Mid-America (100oz)	31	21	18	15	10	15	7		
Total	8,522	9,576	12,863	11,737	12,787	16,663	11,393	10,196	17,680
Equivalent weight of gold (100's tonnes)	25	27	35	32	34	37	26	23	36

Data source: *Gold 1991, Gold 1992, Gold 1993*

WHAT BEARING DOES THE EXCHANGE FUTURES CONTRACT HAVE ON THE GOLD PRICE?

The importance of the relationship between the futures market and the physical or spot market was first discussed in the early 1980s[9], when it was recognised that a small proportion of futures turnover actually came to physical delivery. Subsequent research shows that substantially less than 1% of the volume of the underlying metal traded is actually physically delivered. There are two reasons for this. Firstly, the great majority of the users of the exchange futures contract are speculators, who have no intention of taking physical delivery in the first place. Secondly, one ounce of gold can be traded over and over again, and each time it is traded it is recorded in the turnover figures.

[9] Janeke, Paula, 'Gold: Looking to the Futures', *Financial Mail,* Johannesburg, pp100-101, 27 July 1984

In her initial study of COMEX, analyst Paula Janeke claimed that the bearish or bullish sentiments of speculators was amplified in the futures market simply because the gearing was higher than the physical market and the trading volumes were so much larger[10]. While her observation is still valid, the impact of futures trading on the gold price has been dwarfed by the other financial derivatives that have since emerged. I once tried to correlate the two variables, namely exchange turnover volume and short-term price movements, expecting a relationship between them since the exchanges are being used primarily by speculators and they tend to respond to sharp price movements. A simple statistical test looking for a possible direct relationship came up with nothing of significance. This result is not surprising as turnover could be expected to increase with both price increases and decreases. The higher turnover associated with a price decline would represent speculators going **short**. Conversely, speculators could be expected to go **long** when the price increases and hence a direct statistical relationship could be expected to show very little correlation.

What of the exchange option?

Once the futures contracts were well established, an option contract based on the underlying exchange futures was the logical development. COMEX was the first exchange to launch an options contract, in October 1982. Once again, in contrast to the over-the-counter option, the contract is completely standardised. The COMEX option is for 100 ounces, which provides the holder with the right to buy (call) or sell (put) a COMEX gold futures contract at the stated price on or before the expiration date. The expiration date is linked to the normal months for futures delivery. (See chapter 3 for a detailed discussion of what an option is.) COMEX traded 56,752 options lots during the first year. Other exchanges scrambled to follow suit, but, as with futures, without much success.

The short-lived London Gold Futures Market swiftly followed COMEX, as did the Mid-American Exchange and the American Stock Exchange, but all failed to win popularity. Later the Chicago Mercantile Exchange and the Chicago Board of Trade got to the brink of launching options contracts, only to withdraw at the last moment. The reason, quite simply, was that none of the exchanges had enough turnover in the underlying

---

[10] Ibid

futures contract to justify an associated contract in options.

The resulting pre-eminence of COMEX in options, even more than in futures, stands out in the following table:

Volume of Exchange Options, 1982–1991
– in number of contracts

Thousands

	1982	1983	1984	1985	1986	1987	1988	1989	1990	1991
COMEX (100oz)	57	387	1,433	1,396	1,647	2,080	1,699	1,623	1,932	1,398
COMEX (5 day)										13
ASE (100oz)				36	2					
Mid-America (33.2oz)			0	1	0	0	0	2	2	0
BM&F (250g)					96	177	1,404	6,953	5,999	7,454
Total	57	387	1,433	1,433	1,745	2,257	3,103	8,578	7,933	8,866
Equivalent weight of gold (100's tonnes)	177	1,202	4,456	4,455	5,153	6,514	5,635	6,789	7,511	6,213

ASE = American Stock Exchange

BM&F = Bolsa Mercantil & de Furtoros, Sao Paulo

Data source: *Gold 1991*

The only challenger to COMEX is the Bolsa Mercantil et de Futoros in Brazil, where annual turnover has increased dramatically since its launch in 1986. The non-standard contract size of 250 grammes indicates that it is geared to the local market and it will not gain international acceptance. The sharp rate of growth in turnover is a reflection of the idiosyncratic local market responding to Brazil's virtually endemic inflation and financial crises.

HOW DOES THE COMEX OPTION WORK?

The COMEX contract is offered at a range of predetermined strike prices for a standard COMEX 100 ounce futures contract and at a range of expiry dates. The exchange option is a commodity in its own right. It has a value and can be traded on the exchange many times over before it expires. Although the COMEX option is used by a variety of industry participants, much of the activity is highly speculative. Perhaps only 20% of the COMEX option volume is hedging by regular gold market participants. The balance are those speculators who have no interest in the gold market at all, but are simply trying to profit from the highly leveraged investment vehicle[11].

The ratio of hedging to speculation varies greatly, responding to changes in the gold price and price volatility, which makes it difficult to generalise. During times of rapidly moving gold prices (either up or down), the excitement spreads into the COMEX option pit and the proportion of speculative activity increases dramatically. Conversely, during periods of stable and uninteresting prices, much of the COMEX option business will be executed by professionals in the gold market who may be covering or hedging other bullion positions.

Since under 'normal' circumstances, the speculator is the prominent user of the COMEX, option and trading volumes respond to price and day-to-day volatility. They tend to fall when the price shows little activity, but they can soar with short-term increases in the price. To some extent, the two occur together and tend to reinforce each other so that at times it is difficult to identify the cause and effect. Sharply increasing prices are often associated with sharply higher options turnover. But since both put and call options are traded, the opposite can also be true and a sharply lower price can be associated with high turnover. Incidentally, although the options contract is well established, speculators are more comfortable with buying put options than call options. The ratio of puts to calls traded is estimated to be 3:1. It is an estimate because the total turnover figure does not differentiate between puts or calls or net the two off. It is therefore extremely difficult to assess the net overall position of the exchange option at any one time.

The fact that the speculator is the major user of the exchange option is demonstrated in the way in which turnover can increase for reasons outside the gold market. A good example is the surge of turnover in 1987, mentioned earlier in this chapter. The gold price increase in April of that year was triggered by a sudden increase in the silver price. Futures turnover in both the silver and gold pits in COMEX soared, but this is not where it ended and the excitement spilt over into options. Trading volumes increased by 55% during that month. Turnover in options also increased dramatically after Black Monday in October 1987, when equity markets collapsed[12].

Minimal option turnover comes to physical delivery, perhaps scarcely

[11] Green, Timothy, *The Prospect for Gold: View to the Year 2000*, Rosendale Press, London, 1987
[12] *Gold 1988*, Consolidated Gold Fields Gold Survey, London, 1989

1%. This is no surprise as options are a highly geared paper hedge; rarely does the holder intend to take physical delivery.

Even so, the exchange option is a highly visible instrument, because the trading volume is regularly published. And that leads naturally to the question of how these options influence the gold price. The short answer is – in different ways and at different times, at times adding to price volatility and at other times smoothing out sharp price movements. The crucial factor is the amount of associated delta hedging of options positions. The exchange options, however, cannot be judged here in isolation from the parallel, but much less documented, over-the-counter market in options. For that reason I will leave the discussion on options and the gold price to the section on delta hedging (chapter 4), where the inter-play between exchange and OTC options can also be considered.

WHAT IS THE FUTURE FOR EXCHANGE DERIVATIVES?

Although the exchanges, essentially COMEX, set the pattern for gold derivatives, the real growth since the late 1980s has been in over-the-counter trading in forwards and options. COMEX is the great terminal market, but the expansion has been in what New Yorkers tend to call 'the upstairs stuff', off the floor of the exchange. Although the merger of COMEX with NYMEX will bring all the locals together and may offer economies of scale in administration, it does not mean new exchange products.

Indeed, the interesting aspect of exchange derivatives is that, with the exception of the COMEX five day option launched in 1991, there has been virtually nothing in the way of new product development. Contrast this to the OTC derivative revolution where new products, especially exotic options, are appearing almost on a daily basis.

This is not a criticism of the exchanges. There is good reason why COMEX at least has found little need to revamp its products. They work. A standardised contract is a very necessary one given the make up of the exchanges' client base. The OTC market, which deals one-on-one with individual customers, can afford the luxury of creating a tailor-made product to suit the exact needs of the client. On the exchange floor this would be a logistical nightmare and probably an impossible task for the clearing mechanism. My research into the hundreds of Commodity Trading Advisors has shown very clearly that the majority of these funds, if they are going to participate in the gold market, will almost certainly make use of the exchange derivatives. Bear in mind that most of these funds are committed programme traders and to generate computer buy and sell signals they need standard data on the commodity under consideration. Logically, they make use of COMEX statistics. It stands to reason, therefore, that once they have completed their technical analysis of the public domain data, they will then make use of the very standardised product which they have analysed.

Indeed, the emergence of the CTAs has brought a much needed injection of fresh business to the floor of COMEX. Turnover sagged badly in the early 1990s, touching a low of 6 million contracts in 1991, half of the volume in the record year of 1982. Helped by CTA trading, it is likely to push back over 9 million contracts in 1994.

Inevitably exchange volume fluctuates: in periods of low interest rates, which are good for precious metals because carrying costs are less, it will be up; when interest rates rise, investors and speculators will look elsewhere and turnover on gold (or silver) contracts will decline. But in any event, the exchange derivatives, one might say simply the COMEX derivatives, are firmly placed as an integral part of the gold market.

3

WHAT ABOUT THE OTC MARKET?

The over-the-counter (OTC) or principal-to-principal market is like the *à la carte* menu offered by a rather exotic restaurant. In fact, one can actually take the analogy one step further and say that the OTC restaurant is so geared to its diners that there is no menu. Instead the clientele come in and create their own dishes and menus based on some fundamental raw ingredients. The OTC market now sees most of the derivative activity and it has evolved extremely rapidly in all sectors.

The OTC market is the principals' market whereby business is transacted directly between the buyer and seller. There is no middle-man, exchange or clearing house involved. This market now dwarfs the exchanges, but one of the major problems with analysing it is that it is virtually invisible. Unlike the exchange open interest and turnover figures which are widely available, very little information about the OTC market ever reaches the public domain. There is no regulatory body which insists that data is collated and then made public. So when information does filter through to other market participants, it is normally anecdotal rather than reliable fact. Despite this invisibility it is important to try to understand its presence and influence on the price of gold. So try we must.

WHAT IS THE OTC EQUIVALENT TO THE EXCHANGE FUTURES CONTRACT?

The simple answer is the forward contract, with business conducted directly between the client and the bullion dealers. In gold, the mining companies are the main users.

The forward sale is nothing new, of course, it has been used in precious metals, particularly silver, for generations, but it has come into much wider use by gold mining companies since the mid-1980s. It is a binding contract which cannot be cancelled, although a customer wishing to unwind a sale can do so through a purchase of equal size for the same maturity date.

Unlike exchange futures contracts which are inflexible in their specifications, the principals involved in the forward market today have considerable latitude to tailor forward contracts so that they meet the specific needs of their customers. Consequently, there are numerous types of forward contracts, each with slightly different specifications. The chart appearing in the Appendix (p112) collates the specifications of some of the more commonly used forward contracts. It is designed to show when each product is best used or avoided and the advantages and disadvantages of each. This list is by no means complete, but it is a start.

Transactions are completed through established lines of credit. These agreements are individually negotiated, so consequently margin maintenance is sometimes waived, either in part or in full depending on the credit rating of the counterparty intending to make use of the forward contract. The bigger the mining house, the greater the possibility of them negotiating freedom from margin calls.

WHAT INFLUENCES A COMPANY'S DECISION TO MAKE USE OF THE FORWARD CONTRACT?

Market participants, rightly or wrongly, take for granted that the gold price remains almost permanently in **contango**. A market where the spot price maintains a premium to the forward price (ie, a market in **backwardation**) would indeed be an anomaly for many of the gold market participants. Producer forward sales policies are based on the premise that the gold price will not lapse into a backwardation for periods long enough to influence the nature of those sales policies. Consequently, the decision to sell forward is taken primarily to secure the contango and the spot price. This, however, is a very simplistic explanation of why certain decisions are taken. Forward selling and the structure of hedging programmes that have evolved are based on other interrelated factors[1].

When producers review their hedging strategies they look at five variables:

1   the US dollar price of gold;
2   the cost of borrowing gold;
3   local interest rates;
4   local currency movements against the US dollar;
5   time to maturity (life of the contract).

With the one exception of the time to maturity or the anticipated life of the contract, these variables are usually not considered independently but rather as they influence each other. Items 1 and 4, namely the US dollar price of gold and the local currency's value against the US dollar, are very closely linked. Producers will sell forward when they believe that the price is high and could decline throughout the life of the contract. This applies not only to the gold price in US dollar terms but, more importantly, the price expressed in the producer's local currency. Any weakening of the South African rand or the Australian dollar against the US dollar, for example, may in future imply higher returns in the national currency and so provide the incentive to secure those prices. For this reason, the market need not necessarily see a rally in the US dollar price of gold to experience further producer selling from either Australia or South Africa. Currency movements alone can trigger the implementation of further hedging.

Items 2 and 3, the cost of borrowing and interest rates, are also closely linked. This is because the contango earned by selling forward is the difference between the two (for details, refer to chapter 5 on market liquidity and resulting borrowing costs). Thus if interest rates fall or the cost of borrowing gold rises, the contango earned falls. The converse is also true. Throughout the early 1990s, the sharply reduced contango in response to falling interest rates clearly influenced the North American mining community's decision to hedge. Australian interest rates also fell and reduced the contango in local terms.

---

[1] Jacks, Jessica, 'When? How? and What? Rather than Why?', *Nikkei Research Institute of Industry and Markets Gold Report*, Tokyo, January 1992

Unlike the exchange futures therefore, the structure of which has remained unchanged since its inception in the 1970s, the forward products developed and launched by the OTC market have evolved based primarily on variables 1, 2, 3 and 5. And there are a number of different forward contracts, each with different characteristics, each being essentially a slightly different response to the major variables.

The fixed forward is the standard contract which locks in the spot price of gold at the time of transaction, a fixed interest rate and gold borrowing cost and hence a fixed contango. The date to delivery is also fixed. This is the most basic forward contract and clearly the least flexible. The floating gold rate forward, as the name suggests, keeps all the other variables constant, including the date to maturity, but allows for a variable gold borrowing cost which is then fixed at maturity based on the actual historical costs during the life of the contract. The floating forward gives further flexibility, allowing both the interest rate and the gold borrowing costs to float throughout the life of the contract although the spot price of gold and the date to delivery is fixed at the outset. Once again the two floating variables are fixed at maturity when, with the knowledge of hindsight, actual data is available.

The spot deferred contract allows the most flexibility, so it is no surprise that this product has gained such popularity during the height of producer hedging in the late 1980s and early 1990s. This contract allows not only the interest rate and the gold borrowing cost to float, but also a flexible date to maturity. In other words, the product is designed to be rolled over.

These are some, but certainly not all, of the basic forward products. They allow mining companies to put into practice their views on the five variables. If, for example, interest rates are high and the producers believe that they could come down throughout the life of the contract, they may elect to lock in that interest and consequently the higher contango by making use of the fixed or the floating gold rate forward. Conversely, if mining companies believe that interest rates are likely to rise and therefore they may incur an opportunity cost if they were to lock in those rates, they may elect to use the spot deferred contract. If, during the life of that contract, interest rates were to rise and the contango widen, then the company could convert the spot deferred into a fixed forward and lock in the higher rates. The very same argument applies if the gold borrowing costs were particularly high and expected to fall.

It is not just the five variables that can influence decisions on which forward product to use. The choice of forward contract is also influenced by the particular mining project and its stage of development or production and even its cost structure. The spot deferred contract with its flexible delivery date favours a newly commissioned mine where physical delivery against the existing contract may, for whatever reason, be delayed for a short time. The **flat rate forward**, or **advanced premium forward** (also known as the **stabilised contango**), yet another product, also lends itself to a new project as the contango earned is held constant throughout the contract. This implies that the new mine earns higher returns in the early years at the expense of a lower contango in the later years. This often suits a new project since most of the expenses are loaded into the first operating years.

Taking the development of slightly more intricate hedging strategies a step further, all the various forward products can be used with options. One product that has been marketed aggressively, although with limited success, is the participating forward. This is a basic forward contract with all the variables fixed, but it has a call option associated with it. This then reduces the loss of participation during a rally in the price as the call option would be exercised if the spot price on maturity were to exceed the option strike price. The participating forward may well have advantages over other forward products, particularly if the producer is concerned about the potential loss of upside, or if the gold price is expected to be very volatile.

In all these aggregate products, of course, the buyers get nothing for nothing and there is a cost to every added advantage. Buyers must look for those costs which may be hidden under those apparent advantages. The participating forward, for example, does not earn the miner all or any contango, since it is the contango that pays for the purchase of the options. The option in most cases is a so-called **European-style option** which is exercisable only on the date of maturity. If the option is **out of the money** on that particular day, then it expires worthless and the premium (contango in this case) is lost.

Apart from the advantages or disadvantages of the various products, basic or complex, potential buyers should look closely at the cost of each package. Very often where the basic products have been combined to yield something that may appear to suit the needs of the producer ideally, the result can be very expensive. In other words, the cost of the aggregate product could well exceed the sum of the costs of its individual components.

HOW DO OTC FORWARD CONTRACTS IMPACT ON THE SPOT PRICE OF GOLD?

Forward selling as part of a regular hedging programme for day-to-day price protection results in a distortion of supply projections. The producers enter into a forward contract with the bullion dealer. Since the dealer has taken a potentially long position, he offsets it by borrowing metal from the pool of liquidity and selling this gold into the market. Essentially, the gold price today has to account for production physically present in the market, but yet to be produced, because the borrowed gold is actually disposed of: what the mine produces later goes not to the market but to repay the borrowed gold. This is what is meant when analysts talk about **accelerated supplies** of metal to the market.

Historically, forward selling was completed over a short period of time, usually a three-month rolling schedule. As these positions were regularly unwound, the net impact in a calendar year was minimal and the supply/demand balance was hardly affected. Recently, however, there has been a growing trend among miners to commit sometimes in excess of four or five (even up to ten) years' production to the forward market. These long-dated forwards have had a considerable impact on the current price, particularly during the late 1980s and the early 1990s, far more so than the futures contracts. This is because the bullion dealer accepting the forward transaction usually offsets the total exposure by selling it, normally in a single tranche, into the spot market.

This action has been revealed in a very distinctive way in the behaviour of the gold price. During 1988 and much of 1989, each time the gold price showed any signs of strengthening, producer selling through the forward market effectively placed a ceiling on the price improvement. As the price drifted down throughout most of 1989, the price at which producers were willing to lock in profits also declined and therefore the market price become trapped in narrow trading ranges with well defined ceilings. If this is the case and producers indeed place a ceiling on a price rally by selling forward, should they be doing it? This important question is dealt with separately in chapter 8.

DARE WE ASK ABOUT OTC VANILLA AND EXOTIC OPTIONS?

If you feel a little apprehensive when asking about OTC options, take heart because more often than not, you are in good company. It is this sector that has shown the most spectacular growth not only in terms of the number of products on the market but, more importantly, in terms of their complexity. So it is here that you will find mind boggling strategies and even more outlandish terminology.

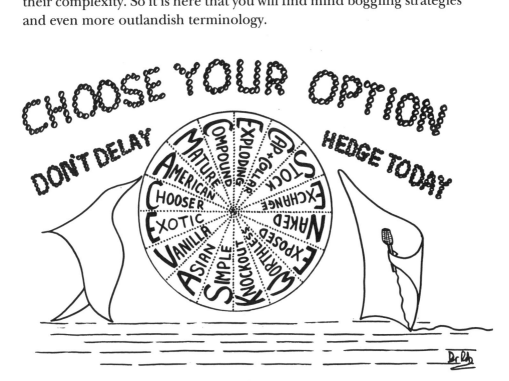

WHAT IS AN OPTION?

An option gives the holder the right without the obligation to buy or sell gold at a predetermined (strike) price by an agreed date. The cost of the option, (premium), represents the compensation the grantor (writer) receives from the buyer for the willingness to grant the option. Options are highly leveraged as the premium is only a small fraction of the total value of the underlying commodity. As a consequence, buyers of options can hold large positions without having to commit substantial amounts of capital to cover the total market value of the exposure.

HOW DOES THE OTC OPTION
DIFFER FROM THE EXCHANGE OPTION?

As the OTC forward contract is to the exchange futures, so the OTC option is the sister product to the exchange option. Where the exchange option is standardised and relatively inflexible, the OTC option gives out the clear message: anything goes!

Apart from flexibility, there are a number of other differences. Bear in mind that this is a private agreement between the buyer and grantor. The buyer stipulates the exact requirements regarding the strike price, date of expiry and quantity. The grantor then quotes a price for this order. Its creation and existence is therefore beyond the jurisdiction of an exchange or its governing body.

Secondly, as it is an agreement between two principals, it is not a publicly tradeable commodity and it can only be exercised or liquidated by the original holder on or before the expiry date. Because of its principal-to-principal nature, it is mainly used by market participants who may require a tailor made product. Finally, grantors of OTC options are not obliged under any regulations to make public the details of any aspect of their options exposure. Indeed, they keep their option dealing as confidential as they would a large physical transaction. It is therefore impossible to assess the size or value of OTC options with any degree of certainty. However, market makers agree that the OTC option is now significantly larger than the exchange option in terms of both volume and value.

The wide acceptance, use and unparalleled growth of the OTC option is a relatively recent development in the gold market. But its origin actually goes back further than one may think. Mocatta Metals Corporation in New York and Valeurs White Weld (now Credit Suisse First Boston Futures Trading) in Geneva introduced OTC options in the late 1970s. It was, however, only during the 1980s that 15–20 international bullion dealers mainly in London, New York and Switzerland, began offering a range of option services[2].

Of this total, only half are considered market makers, as the others act as brokers by offering option services which will ultimately be transacted via the market makers.

---

[2] Green, Timothy, *The Prospect for Gold: View to the Year 2000*, Rosendale Press, London, 1987

The OTC option is now used by many of the major market participants, but it tends not to attract speculative interest in the same volume as the exchange option.

Central banks are increasingly recognising that they can grant OTC call options as a means of earning revenue on their otherwise sterile bullion reserves. Participants in the capital markets, issuing **bonds** backed with gold warrants, can do so by granting options. Throughout the hedging boom of the late 1980s and especially during the early 1990s, mining companies also became very involved in OTC options, using the instrument not only for price protection but also as a means of enhancing their revenue streams. By doing this, it has not limited them to simply buying put options but they have also become substantial grantors of call options, especially as interest rates fell and the contango earned by selling forward declined sharply.

Option books run by the market makers appear to differ in terms of their client bases, making an assessment of the overall industry very difficult. Furthermore, the make up of an option book changes continually with time as options expire and new transactions are initiated. The price at any one time also tends to influence the type of strategy entered into as well as the market participants. For example, the stable and declining prices seen throughout 1988 and most of 1989 encouraged mining companies to make use of certain strategies which were rendered less appropriate during the more volatile and rising prices recorded after November 1990. The higher prices between November and February 1991 attracted a substantial amount of capital market business which subsequently evaporated as gold resumed trading in a lack lustre range. This capital market business returned again during the price rally in the second quarter of 1993 as a number of gold-backed warrants and bonds were launched and marketed into the rising price. (See chapter 6.)

WHAT ARE THE BASIC OPTION STRATEGIES?

All option-based strategies, no matter how complicated, are made up of a combination of two basic transactions called puts and calls.

A **put option** gives the holder the right to sell gold at a predetermined price. The holder then has protection, throughout the life of the option, against a decline in the price without losing the upside potential a higher price may offer. The premium represents the cost to the holder of the option for this price protection. For example, a put may be purchased at a strike price of $400/oz. Should the spot price fall below $400 before the expiry date, the holder may then exercise the right to sell gold at $400. If the gold price remains above $400, the option will expire worthless and the only financial loss to the holder will be the original premium.

A **call option** gives the holder the right to buy gold at a predetermined price. For example, a call may be bought at a strike price of $400/oz. Should the gold price rise over $400 during the life of the option, the holder could exercise the option and buy gold at $400. If the spot price fails to rise over $400, the option would expire worthless and the holder would have lost only the premium paid for the option.

A call option with a strike price below the spot price and a put option with a strike price above the current price is said to be **in the money**. Conversely, calls with a strike price above the current price and puts with a strike price below the spot price are termed **out of the money**. When the strike price equals the spot price, the option is said to be **at the money**. This is a very complicated way of saying: how is your option currently doing? If it is outperforming the gold price and offering you potential profit then it is in the money. If it is losing money relative to the current spot price and

In and Out the Money Options

causing you either some embarrassment or even a sleepless night, then it is out of the money.

There are two components to the value of an option, namely the intrinsic value and the time value. The intrinsic value is the in-the-money difference between the market price of gold and the strike price of the option. The time value is a function of the life of the option because during that time, an option can move in or out of the money. Any value that an option has when the strike price of the option equals the current price of the underlying commodity is time.

OTC options are tradable with the principal market, in other words directly with a bullion dealer. Options that can be exercised only on the maturity date are called **European-style** options. Options that can be exercised at any time before the agreed maturity date are called **American-style** options.

HOW ARE OPTIONS PRICED?

The cost of the option is calculated based on five factors:

1 the strike price of the option;
2 the current price of gold;
3 current interest rates;
4 the time to expiry;
5 the anticipated volatility in the gold price.

The original option pricing theory was developed by Dr Fischer Black and Dr Myron Scholes from data at the Chicago Board of Options Exchange on sixteen commodities and securities, and was later applied to gold. Their Black-Scholes model forms the basis of option pricing, although a number of derivations are in use.

The significant aspect to this is that all the variables associated with option pricing, with the exception of the anticipated volatility, are known. Therefore, option market makers quote prices that are based on very similar calculations; the only input that could differ markedly is the anticipated or implied volatility. Furthermore, the nature of the underlying commodity is not particularly relevant and the model used for pricing gold can also be used to price other options, for example, currency and interest rate options.

The accompanying graphs are profit/loss charts and show hypothetical examples of buying and granting a $410 call and buying and granting a $390 put. They show that the risk associated with buying a put or call option is limited only to the premium paid. This is not the case when granting or writing a put or call option as the loss potential can be unlimited if the price moves against the grantor and the exposure is not hedged. Unhedged options are termed **naked**.

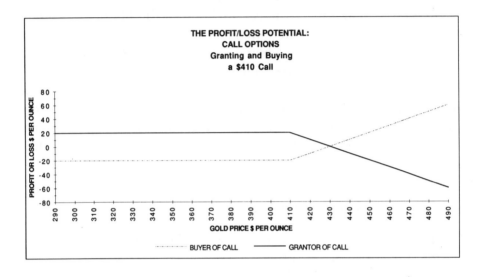

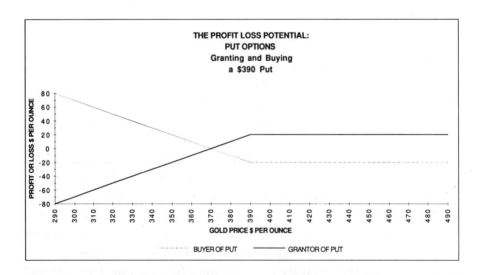

The risks associated with granting naked options were clearly revealed as early as 1985. For several months prior to March 1985, a New York Company, Volume Investors, granted naked but deeply out-of-the-money gold call options to the maximum of 4,000 contracts per trader. While the options remained out of the money, Volume Investors made substantial profits on the premiums earned by the granting of the options. On 18 and 19 March, the gold price rose very sharply from \$290/oz to over \$330/oz and the Volume Investor gold options moved into the money. The company was called on to deliver against their positions and the directors were unable to cover these short positions. Consequently, they failed to pay the required margin and the company defaulted to the sum of \$26 million[3].

Option dealers and market makers, in general, will hedge the options they grant and this tends to be done within the context of their overall option book. There are, however, exceptions to this when options are written and deliberately left naked. Where options are granted in order to earn revenue on an existing long physical position, or granted to offset the costs incurred through buying other options, the positions may not have to be hedged. Furthermore, high risk/reward speculators attempting to profit from the premium earned by granting options may want to take the risk of remaining fully exposed rather than to reduce, through hedging, the revenue on the premium.

The impact of this hedging on the spot price is discussed in chapter 5 on delta hedging.

How big is the OTC option market?

The short answer is: big, very big and getting bigger. The major problem for analysts is that it is virtually impossible to make an estimate that could be considered even remotely accurate. Firstly, the market is enormously secretive. Secondly, it is a moving target and it waxes and wanes with changes in time, price volatility, the spot price and perhaps most importantly the end users of the options. For instance, both mining companies and central banks make use of options from time to time. I sought to gauge their involvement in two annual surveys of the mining industry and one survey of the bullion dealers, asking them about central bank option granting. Both parties responded well, but the surveys, by their very nature, covered only a snapshot of the market, frozen in time. Moreover, there is a constant unknown in the OTC market. We have no idea of the extent of the options books maintained by the

[3] O'Dea, C.R., 'The Guarantee That Wasn't There', *Intermarket*, pp38-45, Chicago, July 1985

bullion dealing community, market makers or others. Not only do the bullion dealers act as counterparts to the end users of options, they are regular end users themselves, taking large option positions on their own account.

WHAT IS A PLAIN VANILLA OPTION AS OPPOSED TO AN EXOTIC OPTION?

The options that I have described so far are affectionately known as plain vanilla options since they are the basic standard product. The exotic options are substantially more fancy in their make up and there are a number of different families of exotic options. The problem with studying the exotics is that they are being created virtually on a daily basis. For the purposes of this book, I do not attempt to describe the exotic options in any detail. Instead, I would rather leave the reader with a general feel for them and I include as many as possible in the glossary of terms.

The **Asian option** is the most basic exotic option. At expiration, the strike price is not compared with the spot price at the time of maturity but rather the average spot price that was achieved throughout the life of the option. This protects the option holder from the concern that I will raise later when I describe how metal trading, just before the moment exchange options mature, can and does influence the short-term spot price.

The Asian option then naturally introduces one of the fundamental differences between the vanilla and the exotic options. The fate of the vanilla option is not dictated by what happens to the price of the underlying commodity during the life of the option.

In contrast, the performance of the spot price throughout the life of most exotic options has very substantial and definitive bearing on what eventually happens to the option. In other words, they are history or path dependent. One of the families of exotic options which most dramatically demonstrates this is the **barrier**, **knock-out**, knock-in or **exploding** family. A knock-out option exists until some pre-agreed barrier in the price is broken and this can happen at any stage of the option's life. When it happens, the option ceases to exist, it explodes, or as John Cleese in the Monty Python TV series would patiently explain, the option is no more, it is deceased, it is an ex-option. You might well ask what possible advantage this option could have over other less heart-rending equivalents. Well, by allowing the option to explode, the holder is surrendering potential time value and therefore the knockout option is sold at a discount to its counterparts.

Not all exotic options are dependent on the price performance of the underlying commodity throughout the option's life. Take for example the **chooser option**. The holder has an option which, at expiry, allows him to choose to which underlying commodity that option relates. In other words, it is like buying a ticket to some entertainment on Saturday night. Come Saturday night (expiration day) and you can choose (preferably before you dress of course) whether you want to go to the ballet or a ball game. Another chooser option gives you an option in gold for example, but at expiry, you can choose whether you want your option to be a put or a call.

In my Nikkei Research Institute of Industry and Markets column one month[4], I took the liberty of creating some of my own exotic options. My favourite, conceived during the dull market of 1992, was a look-back-through-time-to-happier-days option, which got the holder back to the gold price of $850 on 21 January 1980.

While I enjoyed allowing my imagination to run riot, the exercise of creating outlandish derivatives did demonstrate to me that in terms of permutations and combinations of underlying assets and commodities, the sky is indeed the limit. It brought home to me just how and why we have seen such an explosion in the type of products available and the true potential of this market.

---

[4] Jacks, Jessica, 'Opting Out for a While', *Nikkei Research Institute of Industry and Markets Gold Report*, Tokyo, May 1992

4

WHAT IS DELTA HEDGING?

I have now witnessed the same incident three times, in three different gold centres around the world, but each time the outcome has been exactly the same – utter confusion, eyes that glaze over and people shaking their heads in what can only be described as dismay. I am referring, of course, to each time some poor unsuspecting soul has had the courage to ask the question: what is delta hedging? I have never yet heard anyone give a concise, understandable and logical answer to this question. So here it is:

> Delta hedging is a measure of the probability of an option being exercised against the grantor. If the delta is 40%, then 40% of the amount of gold associated with the option must be hedged to negate the exposure. This measure can and does change with time throughout the life of the option. From 40%, it may increase to perhaps 60% and then decline to 20% before the option expires. Each time it changes, the delta hedger adjusts the hedging position accordingly.

I have giving this explanation on a number of occasions and each time the response has then been: 'Fine, we now understand what delta hedging is but we get confused as to who sells what and when that person turns buyer and if they are holders or grantors of **puts** or **calls**.'

This is confusing, but again there is a simple answer, summed up in the following diagram. I personally believe that this diagram is a stroke of genius and I only wish that I could take the credit for its construction. I cannot. All credit goes to Andrew Dowse of Merrill Lynch, London and I am eternally grateful to him, not only for giving me permission to reproduce it in a number of publications, but for sharing it with me in the first place. It explained so much to me, I can only describe the diagram as a revelation. Read it like a train time table and it will tell you exactly who is buying and selling and when.

PUTS

HOLDERS/ BUYERS	IMMEDIATE ACTION	SUBSEQUENT ACTION	
		PRICE RISES	PRICE FALLS
	BUY		BUY
		SELL	

CALLS

HOLDERS/ BUYERS	IMMEDIATE ACTION	SUBSEQUENT ACTION	
		PRICE RISES	PRICE FALLS
			BUY
	SELL	SELL	

PUTS

GRANTORS/ WRITERS	IMMEDIATE ACTION	SUBSEQUENT ACTION	
		PRICE RISES	PRICE FALLS
		BUY	
	SELL		SELL

CALLS

GRANTORS/ WRITERS	IMMEDIATE ACTION	SUBSEQUENT ACTION	
		PRICE RISES	PRICE FALLS
	BUY	BUY	
			SELL

PUTS   CALLS

(With thanks to Andrew Dowse, Merrill Lynch, London.)

There are two very important aspects about this diagram. Firstly, it shows the *theoretical* hedging associated with the delta variable. Secondly, the diagram is symmetrical about its X axis. This implies that for every delta hedge buyer there is an equal and opposite delta hedge seller. Therefore, logic tells us that delta hedging should have no impact on the price of gold. This is true only in theory. In reality, more often than not, delta hedge buying/selling does not generate an equal but opposite response in the market. Therefore, delta hedging can and does have a considerable impact on the short-term price of gold.

Writing an option results in the grantor adopting either a potentially **long** or **short** position. The grantor of a call takes a potentially short position because he has sold someone the right to buy gold from him. Conversely, the grantor of a put takes a potentially long position as he has given someone the right to sell gold to him. The delta variable is a measure used by option participants to calculate the amount of the underlying commodity to be bought or sold in order to hedge the resultant exposure to become what is called delta neutral.

In exactly the same way as options are priced, the delta variable is calculated using a basic computer model which takes into account a number of factors:
- changes in the spot price;
- the time to expiry;
- the differential between the **strike** and spot price.

As the delta changes, the option grantor will therefore protect the exposure by either buying or selling metal depending on:
- the size of the original strategy;
- the grantor's overall option position;
- the direction in which the current price moves relative to the option strike price.

The delta varies between 0 and 1. Deeply **in-the-money** options have a delta close to or equal to 1. The **intrinsic value** of these options changes almost linearly with changes in the current gold price. The delta of a deeply **out-of-the-money** option will be close to or equal to 0 as the option will have little or no intrinsic value. It stands to reason therefore that the further out of the money the options are at the time of granting, the lower the delta variable and hence the less the initial delta hedging associated with the option. Conversely, the closer into the money the options are, the greater the delta hedging. In general, about 50% of the underlying commodity is initially hedged if the options are **at the money.**

In practice, delta hedging may take place as follows: Assume that an option dealer grants 100,000 ounces of out-of-the-money put options at a strike price of $375 while the current price of gold is $400/oz. The option dealer will have sold the holder the right to sell gold to him at $375/oz and therefore will have taken a potentially long position which should be hedged. The delta would then be calculated. For demonstration purposes, the delta may be, say, 0.4. Probably the option dealer will *immediately* sell 40,000 ounces (40%) into the market in order to become delta neutral. This can be done either spot or through a futures contract. The immediate transaction is the primary delta hedging.

Now, if the current price of gold was then to fall towards the put strike price, the chances of the options being exercised against the option dealer would increase. The delta would increase to say 0.45. The option dealer would then have to sell another 5% (5,000 ounces) and so on. This then is the secondary delta hedging. Assuming that the current price was to continue falling to below the strike price, the put options would then be in the money, and the full 100,000 ounces theoretically should have been sold into the market by the time the holder exercised the puts against the option dealer.

Exercising Options

However, after the initial sale of 40,000 ounces, if the puts failed to come into the money because the current price increased, the delta would fall as the probability of the puts being exercised would decline. The option dealer, to remain delta neutral, would then buy gold according to the delta variable. Theoretically, the option grantor should have bought back the full 40,000 ounces as the current price continued rising and the puts fell further out of the money.

The converse is true if the option dealer had granted out-of-the-money calls. The grantor would hedge the resultant short position by buying an initial proportion of the total amount of gold involved. If the delta increased because the gold price increased towards the strike price, the grantor would continue buying gold gradually according to the change in the delta variable. The full amount of the original exposure would then be hedged if the current price equalled or exceeded the strike price and the calls were exercised. The option grantor would sell a proportion of the exposure if the current price and the delta declined as the probability of the options being exercised also decreased.

The above examples demonstrate that the grantor of both put or call options, after the initial tranche of selling or buying respectively, will be a buyer of gold into price rallies and a seller into price falls. The above examples relate to the option grantor. In theory, I could run through the exact opposite transactions conducted by the buyer of these put and call options and you will see that the transactions are completely symmetrical. So much for theory – in reality life is rarely conveniently balanced and symmetrical.

WHY IS DELTA HEDGING OFTEN ONE-SIDED?

There are a number of very valid reasons why delta hedging often fails to meet counter trading and the transaction then becomes one-sided.

Unlike the option grantor, the potential losses incurred by the option holder are limited only to the premium paid for the original option and this often negates the need for the option buyer to delta hedge. The decision whether or not to delta hedge therefore depends on who the option holder is and there are no hard and fast rules about this. If, for example, the options have been bought for price protection by a mining company, that company will not delta hedge the position. Mining companies are naturally long of gold by virtue of their reserves in the ground and their daily production of metal. They therefore should be in a position to deliver against their options if they were ever exercised. Hence there is no need for them to delta hedge.

Often options are granted with the specific intention of gaining the revenue represented by the option premium. A very good example of this was seen in the early 1990s when central banks began granting call options against a proportion of their gold reserves. By doing so, they began to earn a return, often an attractive one, on what was otherwise a non-interest bearing asset. If the central banks then delta hedged their position, they would merely have eroded their revenue, which would have defeated the whole purpose of granting the options in the first place. Therefore they took a calculated risk, intentionally leaving themselves exposed for a proportion of their reserves. Some got away with it as their options remained out of the money and were never exercised against them. A few central banks had exposure in the market where the price rose sharply in 1993 and had to deliver gold against their options. Apparently these central banks were not particularly concerned about 'losing their gold to options'. At the time of granting the options, they had allocated a certain amount of gold to the option programme in the full knowledge and understanding that the options may result in them parting with their metal.

The rate at which the delta changes is not linear. With deeply in-the-money or out-of-the-money options, the delta variable is not sensitive to changes in the gold price. However, the closer an option is to being at the money, the more price elastic the delta variable becomes. This non-linear relationship complicates the delta hedging of a large option book since options will have been granted and bought at a wide range of strike prices, some at the money and others deeply out of the money. Some option positions will therefore require frequent incremental hedging during their lives while others will not. Option dealers overcome this by measuring the rate of change of the delta (the gamma) and calculate the overall gamma position of the book which is then hedged.

Apart from the delta and the gamma, there are other measures of option exposure. The vega, for example, is a measure of a change in volatility in the gold price and what this change could mean for the existing option exposure. The theta calculates a change in that option exposure that results from the passage of time.

How do options
impact on the spot price of gold?

The extensive use of OTC options which could give rise to short, medium and long-term price influences is still too new to gold to give a final, definitive answer to this question. However, it is fair to say that even with the limited experience so far, options can influence the gold price.

This same question has been applied to other option-related markets and analysts can try and draw parallels from these experiences. In 1986, the Bank of International Settlements published the results of a study group which addressed this issue as it related to currencies and interest

market, the option dealers were selling a proportion of gold associated with the puts they had granted but, at the same time, were buying a proportion of the gold associated with the call options they had bought from the mining company. The extent to which one transaction offset the other depended on the ratio of puts sold to calls bought and their position within the overall option book.

In contrast, the mining companies tended not to hedge either the put options they bought or the call options they wrote. The puts were bought specifically for price protection and there was very little need for them to be hedged. As far as the writing of the calls was concerned, in theory, the mining companies ought to have maintained a delta neutral position. But miners, by nature, hold a long gold position as they have proven reserves in the ground. The need to delta hedge the call options therefore was negated to some extent because the mine could provide gold from production to meet the calls if they were exercised. The net outcome was that the mining companies, through all their hedging programmes, including options, established potentially short positions in the market.

This situation prevailed until the price increased in November when it suddenly broke through \$400/oz and tested \$410/oz. Anecdotal evidence suggests that the mining companies decided to cover some of their short positions and entered the market as buyers. This is believed to be one of the reasons why the price increased to over \$420/oz. Once the short positions were covered, the upward pressure on the price diminished.

The second example of OTC options fuelling short-term volatility concerns the capital markets. Shortly after the price began increasing in November 1989, there were numerous bond issues with attached gold warrants launched in the capital markets. The gold component of the bonds was typically in the form of call options. These calls represented a potentially short position held by the issuing banks and were delta hedged by buying gold in the market. This, too, contributed to short-lived but upward pressure on a price that was already very volatile. Once the initial hedging had been completed, the upward pressure on the price declined. This occured originally in 1989, but the market exhibited exactly the same behaviour in 1993 when it was suddenly subjected to yet another spate of warrant issues, most of which were associated with call options, which were also similarly delta hedged. Again the warrants helped to fuel a price rally.

So much for the price rallying. What happened when the price softened? Well, all the delta hedge buying associated with the warrants, gradually turned into secondary delta hedge selling and the exact converse was put in place. The faster the price fell, the more the option grantors sold and hence encouraged the price to fall even further.

So, delta hedging is a double edged sword. It can be instrumental in pushing the gold price up or down and it can encourage a sharp movement in either direction. At other times, it can also help smooth out the peaks and the troughs.

Delta hedging, of course, does not eliminate risk completely. If the gold price varies more than the option grantor expected, the hedging required to remain delta neutral could be substantial and the costs incurred could exceed the premium earned from those options.

One final point to bear in mind is that the Black-Scholes model and all the derivations of that original work assume that the price of the underlying commodity is normally distributed. Many argue that this is a basic and fundamental flaw in option pricing. However, until other models are generated which take into account that price distributions over time may not be normal, these models remain the accepted methods of option pricing. Since most option evaluators are using very similar methods, the option pricing is directly comparable. The introduction of a vastly different pricing model could herald a major watershed in option theory, affecting all the underlying commodities and not just gold.

5

WHAT IS THE POOL OF GOLD LIQUIDITY?

In parallel with the gold that is bought and sold daily, there is a substantial lending or leasing market. This metal is used for short-term borrowing and the return is an obvious way of gaining interest on what would otherwise remain a sterile asset.

This pool of liquidity is the life blood of many of the derivatives, without which they simply could not exist. As the bullion dealers complete a derivative transaction, they hedge their exposure to that position. Consequently they normally draw metal from the pool of general liquidity. This applies to most bullion related paper transactions, whether they are **forward sales** or **gold loans** originating from the primary industry option strategies for their own trading book. So it stands to reason that the less metal available for borrowing, the more difficult and expensive it becomes to complete a transaction of this nature.

WHERE DOES THIS METAL COME FROM AND WHERE DOES IT GO?

The official sector is the major source to this lending market simply because the central banks hold large inventories which can be mobilised at short notice. However, dealers or even any private individuals holding metal can and do participate. The primary borrowers of liquidity include the mining industry selling forward and gaining the **contango** via the bullion dealers. In addition, the dealers themselves and also the jewellery fabricators are important participants.

The cost of borrowing responds to both the level of supply and demand for borrowed metal and I consider the cost of borrowing as a primary indicator of the state and the size of the pool of liquidity.

HOW BIG IS THIS MARKET RELATIVE TO OTHER SECTORS?

This is a difficult question to answer because the size of the pool can and does vary almost constantly. I have seen a number of estimates, but remember that analysts are obliged to make estimates of a moving target. In mid-1992, I estimated that the pool was anything between 800 and 1,000 tonnes. Other observers have offered different estimates. American Precious Metals Advisors (APMA) in early 1993 quoted a much higher figure of 4,000–6,000 tonnes[1], a figure that has been questioned. A more moderate quantity of 2,000–2,500 tonnes has been suggested by another report[2]. Since the bullion community keeps confidential the level of its own activities, the true figure must remain open to debate.

However, there is another way of arriving at an acceptable estimate. Research into the total amount of gold associated with the outstanding derivatives from the mining companies gives a reasonable indication of the level of borrowings there. If you make further allowance for the metal borrowing capacity of the jewellery fabricating industry, a fuller picture begins to emerge. Fortunately, this method allows for a cross-check. Once the total figure is estimated, it can then be compared with prevalent borrowing costs to ensure that the two variables are broadly in line with each other. I consider this to be a valid approach since there is an inverse

[1] Nichols, J., 'MetalsFax', American Precious Metals Advisors Inc, USA, 4 January 1993
[2] Cox, I., Report for the World Gold Council, 1993

relationship between the two. The greater the pool of liquidity, the lower the cost of borrowing. Conversely, the less the amount of gold visible in the system, the higher the expected borrowing costs and the more expensive it will for someone to borrow metal.

The pool of liquidity is substantially more significant in the analysis of derivatives than of the physical market, because the flow and availability of borrowed metal lubricates the derivative market, assisting the depth of gold loan, forward and options activity. Without this liquidity, I have no doubt that derivatives would not have evolved as fully or rapidly. This is probably one of the major reasons, incidentally, why the derivative revolution has not encroached as much on the platinum group metals (PGMs), where a good deal of annual mine supply is tied to long-term contracts with major automobile manufacturers. The PGM market also has less metal available in the form of above ground stocks, so the pool of liquidity is best described as a little puddle left by a spring shower.

WHAT ELSE DO WE NEED TO KNOW ABOUT THE COST OF BORROWING GOLD?

A simple mathematical relationship exists between the cost of borrowing metal and the contango earned by the mining industry selling forward.

Pool of Liquidity

The contango earned by the mining companies is the difference between the prevalent money market interest rate and the cost of borrowing gold (less the dealer's commission). It makes sense, therefore, to deal with these components of the industry together.

The cost of borrowing gold or the rate of return for those lending gold into the short-term market influences the volume of metal available. Historically, there was no formalised reporting of the lease rate or the contango and a reliable data series was not easy to come by. This situation was remedied in July 1989 when a dozen market makers began contributing to **GOFO**, a Reuters screen quoting daily gold forward rates. These rates now give a very good indication of the state of the pool of gold liquidity and the GOFO page is now one of the standard sources of reliable gold market information.

The accompanying graph shows on a monthly basis the average gold borrowing costs from January 1982 up until June 1994, expressed in basis points.

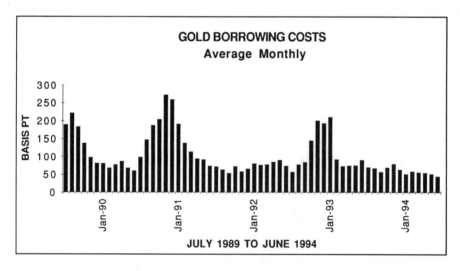

Data calculated from the Reuters GOFO page.

Even with its brief history, the GOFO data has provided useful insights into the workings and state of the pool of gold liquidity. Borrowing costs clearly respond to pressures within the gold market and this in turn influences the contango earned by selling forward. Both the cost of borrowing gold and the contango have important hedging implications for the mining companies and the way they respond has bearing on the price of gold.

So far changes in the cost of borrowing gold have come mainly from the supply side. However, this need not always be the case. In future, demand from borrowers could determine the cost. Substantial levels of forward sales or a resurgence in demand for bullion financing through **gold loans** could well push up the cost of borrowing gold.

The sharp increase in the cost of borrowing gold in late 1990, which is very clear from the graph, provides a clear example of how a withdrawal of central bank gold can influence the rates.

On 9 May 1990, Drexel Burnham Lambert filed for Chapter 11 status in the United States. At that time, their commodity trading arm had central bank gold on deposit, mainly from the Bank of Portugal. While the Bank of England ensured that all contracts entered into with Drexel's United Kingdom subsidiary, which was solvent, were honoured, there remained important implications for the central banks involved. Essentially, the Bank of Portugal was obliged to join the rest of Drexel's creditors in the hope of salvaging a proportion of the value of their exposure to the company. This situation alarmed the central banking community and many withdrew (some only temporarily) their metal from the pool of liquidity. This contraction of lending by the central banks placed sharp upward pressure on the cost of borrowing gold. Interestingly, however, the impact was not seen immediately. The reason cannot be confirmed completely because of the secrecy of the gold market. But the shortfall was almost certainly made up to a large extent by the substantial levels of Russian **swaps** that were completed early in the same year. As part of the swap transaction, the Soviets' counterparts held Russian gold as collateral and this immediately provided another source of metal to the lending market. Only when the Soviets unwound their swaps during the course of the year, did less metal become available, thereby placing pressure on the borrowing costs some time after the Drexel debacle. In short, the Soviet gold cushioned the effect for a while.

The chart also shows that at the end of 1992, the cost of borrowing metal again responded sharply to another withdrawal of gold from the lending market. In the middle of November of that year, I began questioning why this should be the case[3]. All that I could suggest at that stage was that

---

[3] Jacks, Jessica, 'Why is the Pool of Liquidity Drying Up?', *Nikkei Research Institute of Industry and Markets Gold Report*, Tokyo, November 1992

the narrow trading range exhibited by the price implied that there were few speculators who may have gold currently in the leasing market. By a process of elimination, the principal lenders had to be the central banks. An alternative explanation was that this pressure on borrowing costs had to do with the European currency crisis. Perhaps Britain, Spain and Italy, having spent many millions of sterling, pesetas and lira attempting to support their currencies, felt the need to consolidate their reserve bases. If they had any gold in the lending market, withdrawing it and bringing it back into reserves might have been one strategy. I was wrong. Apparently the Netherlands' central bank had withdrawn leased gold from the market in preparation for their sale of a little over 400 tonnes.

These high borrowing costs implied that the lending market at the end of 1990 and again in 1992 was tight and illiquid. This then influenced the economics of the bullion derivative products. As the cost of borrowing gold increases towards money market rates, the economics of a gold loan for a mining company begins to look less and less attractive. Theoretically there comes a time, therefore, when there is no financial incentive to borrow gold as opposed to borrowing dollars. However, this is only part of the full picture. High rates of borrowing also affect mining companies who are not financing capital expenditure through a gold loan. The higher the cost of borrowing, the less the contango earned by mining companies who may wish to make use of the forward market. The following chart shows clearly how the contango has performed since January 1982.

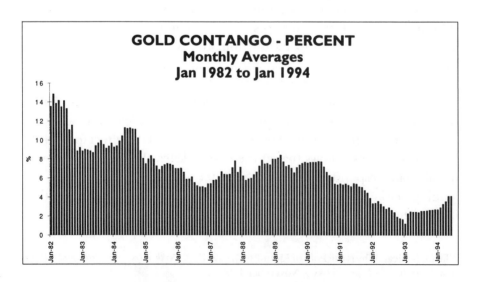

The steady, and indeed very respectable, contango available to the mining industry throughout the mid to late 1980s provides the answer to why we saw so much in the way of forward selling and gold loan draw downs during that period. In short, the mining companies achieved a very good forward price. But then, as interest rates began to soften, the situation changed.

The gradually declining contango after mid-1990 was a factor which caused the mining companies to review their hedging policies. This cause and effect is still valid. Their response, however, is more complicated than simple withdrawal from the forward market. The mining companies have the alternative of adjusting their hedging decisions and making use of other different forward products and options.

One interesting response to the lower contango is that it encourages companies to commit themselves to longer dated contracts where the lower earnings are compounded over a longer period of time. By doing this, they achieve that same price although they lock their product into a specific price for a longer period. The lower contango therefore tends to prompt the greater use of long dated contracts.

The borrowing costs give valuable insights into other relationships within the gold market. On a monthly basis, the cost of borrowing gold versus the spot price yields a strong inverse correlation. This is shown in the following graph which goes back monthly to January 1982.

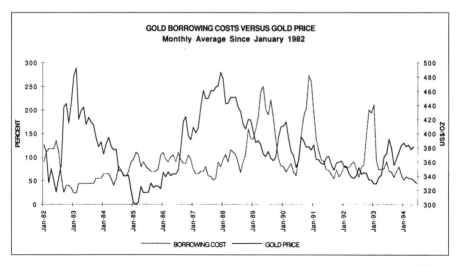

Data source: A. Smith, Union Bank of Switzerland, London. With permission.

Outwardly, this relationship may appear surprising, mainly for two reasons. Firstly, it is unusual for there to be such a strong correlation between two variables in a dynamic market that is often blurred by background noise and other factors influencing them, especially when one variable is the price. Secondly, I did not expect an inverse relationship, but the exact opposite. My rationale was as follows: When the spot price of gold is rising sharply, it becomes increasingly more expensive for the users of gold to purchase their raw material. In the case of gold, the users are primarily jewellery fabricators and they need gold on a regular basis. They would then borrow metal while the price was rising in the hope that by the time they next needed their raw material, the price would have weakened. Given the number of jewellery fabricators who could unconsciously act collectively in this way, it could be expected that the cost of borrowing gold would increase as the spot price rose.

The data, however, disproved my logic[4]. Discussions with dealers showed that the answer lies, not in the demand for leased gold but in the supply to the lending market. As the spot price begins to rise rapidly, it attracts speculative buying. Once these positions are established, the holders of that gold place the metal on short-term deposit in an attempt to earn a return on their investment. This only serves to add to the pool of gold liquidity and logically places downward pressure on the cost of borrowing.

These discussions also showed that the argument concerning the behaviour of the fabricating jewellers was correct in that they do tend to borrow gold rather than buy it when the price is increasing. But apparently, the level of their borrowing nowhere near meets the volume of potential lending and their influence is more than counterbalanced by the amount of gold placed on deposit. Hence, the strong inverse relationship.

This explanation revealed another relationship of interest. The gold price dictates the type of market participant active in the lending market at any time. A dull and lacklustre gold price suggests that the lenders of gold are primarily the central banks. But as the price begins to move up sharply, the ratio of central bank lenders to speculators begins to fall.

The spot price has a direct influence on the cost of borrowing metal. Whether or not the converse is true is less obvious. In other words, how does pressure on the borrowing costs influence the spot price?

---

[4] Ibid

I feel that there should be some influence although perhaps not as clear-cut and direct as its converse. Consider speculators who are currently holding physical metal and have already lent that gold into the market. They have contributed to the overall pool of liquidity and influenced the cost of borrowing. If they now intend to sell the metal, it seems logical that they first have to give notice to the leasing market of the intention to withdraw the gold. Depending on the size of that position and given that the pool of liquidity is not as large as one may think, these actions could place upward pressure on the borrowing costs, which could be an early warning of an intention to liquidate, therefore placing downward pressure on the spot price. This only appears to hold true if a market participant withdraws gold from the lending market with the express intention of selling the metal. If there is no intention of liquidating the position but the participant still withdraws from the lending market, then I see no reason why the borrowing costs should affect the spot price.

AND WHAT ELSE ABOUT THE CONTANGO?

The contango is simply the difference between the spot price and a forward price when the spot price is lower than the forward price. The contango takes into account the cost of carrying and financing metal for future delivery and usually reflects prevalent interest rates.

Because of the level of above-ground stocks of gold, which ensures that the forward market is always liquid enough for trading to take place, the gold price normally remains in contango. Only momentarily has the gold price ever slipped into backwardation, that is when the spot price exceeds the forward price. This occurred very briefly during the sale of central bank gold by the Netherlands in late 1992, although the backwardation was only seen in the overnight rates and certainly not in the three, six or twelve months figures. However, unlike the base metals, a backwardation in gold rarely survives for very long. This is because many market participants hold physical metal and the guaranteed profit through selling spot and buying forward almost instantaneously forces an adjustment of the two prices, and gold reverts back to a contango market. It is therefore the arbitrage opportunities available to those with a natural long gold position that tends to keep gold in contango. This is where gold differs from the base metals, which can and do remain in backwardation for prolonged periods. During times of very high metal demand for industrial consumption, the above ground stocks of base metals can be so low that dealers simply do not have the metal to take advantage of the arbitrage opportunities provided by a backwardation.

6

Gold-backed Bonds, Warrants & Gold Loans

Three gold-related products – gold-backed bonds, warrants and gold loans have been associated with the capital markets, each being developed in response to particular market circumstances.

Gold-backed bonds and **warrants**, which structurally can be fairly complex, are simply a means of raising finance. In this sense, they are very similar to gold loans. While the two methods achieve similar ends, they do have marked differences. Gold loans are a principal-to-principal agreement, involving only two counterparties. Gold-backed bonds offer direct investment opportunities to the public and can be issued with long maturity dates. These bonds have often been a feature of the Swiss market, but they have also been launched in Euromarkets, while recent issues have emanated from North America.

The rationale behind the concept of 'gold-backed paper' is to take advantage of gold's assumed counter-cyclical behaviour. So, when all other investment alternatives are under-performing and markets may be in turmoil, the gold price rises – at least in popular theory. Hence the expectation that these bonds provide the investor with an exposure to gold as a natural hedge if equity markets or other bonds fall sharply. The holder of a gold-backed security has the exposure to potential movements in the gold price, but unlike when holding physical metal, the investment is simultaneously interest bearing.

The gold component can be introduced in a number of ways. Some bonds are convertible into the equity of the issuing gold mining company, others can be converted into physical gold. The most common issues in the mid-1990s are bonds which carry a warrant to buy gold. The warrant, slightly more intricate than the the ordinary bond, is, more often than not, simply a call option, but has the advantage of being a securitised instrument. A spate of bonds each with a warrant (usually an option) to buy a basket of both precious and base metals has also been issued.

First let us look at the convertible bonds, characterised by maturity dates of up to ten years. In the mid-1980s, these maturity dates probably would have been considered extremely long indeed. Since then, however, with a deep and liquid forward market extending commonly out to six and seven years, and with the ability to span a decade, this is no longer the case.

The bond component offers the holder a specific rate of return (often termed the coupon) throughout the life of the investment. The sweetener is the option to convert the investment into an agreed amount of gold, or the cash equivalent on or before the maturity date. At the time of offer, the issuing company stipulates the price at which the gold could be converted and therefore it can hedge this exposure throughout the life of the bond. In this respect, the convertible bond is very similar to a gold loan as the price achieved for the metal at the time of draw down is also known and can be hedged. However, where the interest rate associated with loans has historically ranged from 1–3%, the coupon applicable to bonds in the earlier years was higher. In later issues, the coupon was comparable to interest rates because the coupon is essentially a function of money market rates and the yield on similar investments, while the gold loan interest rates are more a function of the cost of lending gold incurred by the commercial bank involved. Bonds have also been issued with a zero coupon which seems to negate one of the major incentives for investing in the bond in the first place.

WHAT HAPPENED WITH THE GISCARD BOND?

The most widely publicised convertible bond was the Giscard bond, briefly the topic of much market speculation before it matured in 1987[1]. While the Giscard is no longer topical and largely forgotten, it worth reviewing since it highlights how analysts can misinterpret developments and draw erroneous conclusions about a bond's influence on the price.

The bonds were issued in 1973 and expired on 16 January 1988; there were 6.5 million in all and the interest rate (coupon) was 7%. At the time of issue, an indenture was included stating that, in the event of the currency no longer being linked to gold, the bond's coupon would be indexed directly to the gold price. This indenture came into force in 1978 as the currencies of the IMF members lost their gold-related definitions.

When the Giscard reached maturity, the holder of each bond was entitled to the French franc value of 102.07 grams (3.28oz) of gold. Theoretically, this represented a total of 663.5 tonnes of gold (6.5 million bonds × 3.28oz/32,151oz). Rumours abounded in the gold market that the French government would be obliged to buy this amount of metal, or part of it, in the market to cover potential exposure. A price increase in late 1987 was even anticipated because the gold involved represented 26% of the country's gold reserves.

During the last 10 years of the bond's life, a brisk secondary market for the bonds developed and the Giscard traded in line with the gold price, although sometimes the bond changed hands at a steep discount. This occurred, it seemed, when the authorities tried to amend the terms of the issue retro-actively. The whole project became the subject of intense political debate. Domestic tax laws also provided an incentive for the local institutional investors to liquidate their bond holdings before maturity, therefore compounding the discount. Towards the end of the bond's life, arbitrageurs, who believed that the terms of the bond issue would remain unchanged, made full use of the discount by locking in risk-free profit. This was done by selling gold forward or spot, equal to the amount associated with the purchased bonds. In other words, they adopted a long bond-short gold position.

Some analysts assumed that these investors, whom they calculated might be short gold by as much as 133 tonnes, would also need to cover before the expiry date, thus further stimulating the price. It turned out to be a non-event; plenty of smoke but no fire. Not only did these technical short positions fail to materialise, but the French government also

[1] O'Connell, Rhona, *Annual Review of the World Gold Industry 1988*, Shearson Lehman Hutton Inc, London 1988

correctly judged that most bond holders would take cash rather than gold. A mere five tonnes was called for delivery. The final price, by the way, was calculated by averaging the Paris Bourse gold fix for the last 30 trading days of 1987, which came out at $486.67, up nicely on the price of $97.22 in 1973 when the bond was issued.

The final months of the Giscard debate actually co-incided with the first real flurry of new gold-backed bonds with warrants. The issues have largely been during the period of a rising gold price, thus giving the retail end of the investment sector a chance to participate in a perceived bull market. There were 17 bond issues during the price surge between January and September 1986, followed by another 49 issues between January and November 1987 when the price rallied from $400 an ounce to around $460 (helped by substantial buying by the central bank of Taiwan and the much touted Giscard covering). Thereafter, as the price declined below $370 in 1988–89, the bond/warrant market was remarkably quiet – a mere two issues. The price run-up prior to the Gulf war in 1990, however, saw 27 new bond launches. Then things went quiet until the rally of 1993 took gold back from the doldrums of $330 towards $400 and at least 14 new bond issues emerged.

An intriguing factor is that this gold-backed paper, unlike gold loans, has not been confined to the mining companies or the gold industry in general. Industrial companies far removed from the gold market have launched gold bonds. They include AT&T, General Motors, Hoffman La Roche and General Electric, besides banks and government agencies. The presence of these non-gold industries signals one thing; as with the Giscard in the end, very little or no physical gold is involved, settlement is assumed to be in cash, but against the bench-mark of gold. So it is not a sign that General Electric has suddenly entered the gold market as such.

The later gold-backed issues also sought to broaden their appeal. Bonds rather similar to unit trusts (mutual funds) have been offered with a call option covering a basket of commodities including gold, but also base metals. Does this mean that gold bonds alone have been a disappointment compared to other investments?

An exact appraisal of the performance of so many bonds is not practical here; each in turn would need to be compared with the return on other interest-bearing investments, not only in terms of the yield, but also the cost. Suffice to say that a general analysis of many of the gold bonds with warrants launched in 1986–87 showed that they underperformed in relation to other investments. First, the holder accepted a discounted coupon because the accrued interest lagged the prevalent returns on other investments. Second, when the majority of the issues passed their maturity date, the warrant or option was **out of the money** and therefore expired worthless. With no profit from the warrant, many bond holders not only received a poor return on their investment, but also incurred a loss. A further disappointment on these bonds is that a secondary market in which investors could liquidate their holdings if they wish did not really develop.

Yet, the fascination with gold warrants persists. During 1993 alone at least 14 new issues were made, listing more than 20 million ounces (622 tonnes) of call warrants, with a further 3 million ounces (93 tonnes) of put warrants[2]. By no means were these issues fully taken up, but in Europe in particular, many investors did subscribe precisely because of that urge to be on board what looked like a new bull market. And that leads us directly to the next question.

HOW DO THESE ISSUES
IMPACT ON THE SPOT PRICE?

In terms of analytical perils, as the Giscard showed, the gold-backed paper issues offer a sobering lesson. No analyst should simply do the arithmetic and extrapolate the tonnages out – it will prove very misleading indeed. If you do this even for the short period 1973 to 1994, you get the following answer:

Theoretical Tonnage of Gold Associated with the Gold-backed Bonds

	tonnes	cumulative
1973	663.1 (Giscard)	663.1
1984	3.1	666.2
1985	0.0	666.2
1986	20.4	686.6
1987	149.0	835.6
1988	6.8	842.4
1989	56.0	898.4
1990	32.7	931.1
1991	0.0	931.1
1992	0.0	931.1
1993	715.0	1,646.1
1994	250.0*	1,896.1

*Minimum as of end of first quarter

[2] *Gold 1993*, Gold Fields Mineral Services, London, 1994

It is erroneous to suppose that this cumulative amount of gold associated with the capital markets was physically hedged in the bullion market.

However, these bonds can give rise to arbitrage opportunities throughout their life, particularly where a brisk secondary market for the bonds develops. In the case of the Giscard bond, the trend was to sell gold short. Although in the final analysis this did not cause a price squeeze, in theory the potential was there for a sharp rise in the price as these short positions could have required covering. The Giscard also demonstrated that bond issuers do not have to, and indeed tend not to, cover themselves for the full amount of the underlying commodity. This gives rise to a further short position, which may have to be covered suddenly and therefore provides the potential for a short-lived price squeeze.

The way in which bonds with attached warrants impact on the spot price differs from the convertible bonds. Bonds convertible into cash or gold equity have no influence on the gold price, save perhaps for some short-lived and irrational market sentiment. Historically, bonds convertible into physical metal also have little impact since investors have tended to opt for the cash alternative.

This then leaves bonds with attached warrants. Warrants are usually simply gold call options giving the holder the right to buy gold at a predetermined price. The grantor of the warrants therefore ought to delta hedge the exposure by buying an initial tranche of gold. As the gold price increases the grantor should then continue buying according to gradual changes in the delta variable but should sell gold if the price were to fall.

This is exactly what appears to have happened during the period November 1989 to January 1990 and certainly again in 1993. Looking back to 1989, the data suggests that some 90 tonnes of gold were associated with the bond issues over that period. Some of the warrants were **out of the money** and therefore the initial delta hedging was in the order of 40% of the volume of the underlying gold. However, some of the options were **in the money,** therefore necessitating a much greater amount of hedging, perhaps anything from 60–70% of the underlying gold. While I cannot prove this, delta hedging was one reason why the price increased further and faster than otherwise may have been the case during the closing months of 1989[3]. Correspondingly, when the price

---

[3] Jacks, Jessica, 'Gold Options', Ibid

weakened in February and March 1990, the associated delta hedge selling, while significantly less than the original buying, did however further exacerbate the decline in the price.

WHAT OF THE GOLD LOAN?

The gold loan might be described as the most notorious of the derivatives related to gold, not because of its complexity or leverage but simply because of its timing. The gold loan's entrance into the market in a volume that was sufficient to influence the gold price during the late 1980s attracted a good deal of media attention and effectively brought to the fore the whole question of derivatives and their impact on the gold price. The emergence of the gold loan was no co-incidence. A number of market factors came together to create the ideal climate.

The concept of borrowing and lending metal to fund work in progress was certainly not new to the gold market. Gold has been lent out to jewellery fabricators since at least the 1960s. The crucial issue here, however, is not gold loans to fabricators but the borrowing of metal to raise capital to finance large mining projects. The high price of the early 1980s encouraged the exploration for, and development of, dozens of new gold mines, especially in North America and Australia. The gold rush was spurred on by the application of technologies which enabled very low grade deposits to be mined profitably for the first time. These projects required financing and provided a natural market for the development of bullion financing. But why bullion financing? Essentially, the decision to borrow metal as opposed to borrowing dollars resulted from prevailing high interest rates. The differential between the cost of borrowing gold and that of conventional financing proved just too attractive to ignore. In a relatively short space of time, during the mid-to-late 1980s, gold loans rapidly became a common method of raising capital.

As a new phenomenon, no one was really tracking gold loans accurately at first. So, their sudden presence and their implied impact on the price was much debated and lead to a good deal of misconceptions and confusion. Exaggerated statistics were circulated and some market observers initially claimed that gold loans did not influence the underlying supply/demand balance. The majority of participants now accept that gold loans, used to raise capital for financing, represent accelerated supplies of gold to the market and distort the conventional mine supply forecasts. Most supply/demand balances now take gold loans into account.

Unlike other financial derivatives of gold, good statistical information about gold loans is readily available, so analysis and the construction of a detailed data base is possible. The primary sources of reliable data are company annual accounts and **10K reports**, but the bullion banking community and the mining companies themselves have been forthcoming and very co-operative. The amount of gold associated with these loans should be included in a supply/demand balance and any developments should be accounted for when assessing the market. Failure to recognise this results in insufficient insight into the gold market and an inability to satisfactorily explain short-term price movements.

HOW DOES A GOLD LOAN WORK?

In the simplest example, a mining company draws down a gold loan by borrowing bullion from a commercial bank. Usually, the commercial bank will have borrowed bullion from a central bank. The gold is sold in the market to raise the capital necessary to finance the development of a new mine or the expansion of an existing operation. The size of the loan depends on the amount of capital required, although about one year's planned output appears to be the industry average. The gold can be sold into the spot market but, more commonly, it is used to honour a forward contract entered into before the loan draw down. Either way, the market has to absorb this gold over a relatively short space of time and this places downward pressure on the price.

Until the mid 1980s, the use of gold loans was limited; so little gold was involved that the effect on the supply/demand balance and the price was virtually non-existent. However, from 1985 onwards, with the cost of borrowing gold at 4–5 percentage points lower than the cost of borrowing dollars, the gold loan industry developed rapidly and loans were completed in sufficient quantity to become a major influence on the price. While the loans were raised primarily to finance new mines, some were initiated to raise capital for the expansion of existing operations, for acquisition and, in the 1990s, in order to reschedule debt. Less commonly, loans have also been drawn down to boost cash liquidity during balance sheet management[4]. However, the ultimate reason behind the gold loan boom in 1988 (the peak year) was the collapse of the world's

[4] Turner, David, 'Recent Developments in Bullion Financing', Proceedings from the IPMI Annual Conference, Boston, 1988

equity markets on Black Monday, 19 October 1987. In the uncertainty that followed, mining companies clearly felt uncomfortable raising money through the equity markets. Gold loans provided a convenient and relatively cost effective alternative[5].

The accompanying table shows the chronological distribution of the gold loan industry covering the period 1981–94. These statistics are the summary of research and data base work undertaken over a period of several years. Details of a number of the loans are considered confidential and therefore only this summary table has been published[6].

Summary of the Gold Loan Industry

	No of new loans	New draw downs (tonnes)	Known paybacks (tonnes)	Draw downs less paybacks (tonnes)	Nett outstanding loans cumulative (tonnes)
1981	1.0	0.5	0.0	0.5	
1982	1.0	0.4	0.1	0.3	0.8
1983	0.0	0.0	0.1	–0.1	0.7
1984	4.0	3.4	0.1	3.3	4.0
1984	20.0	39.2	1.0	38.2	42.2
1986	13.0	23.9	6.0	17.9	60.1
1987	37.0	72.9	14.8	58.1	0.0
1988	92.0	181.2	23.8	157.4	157.4
1989	58.0	164.3	65.2	99.1	256.5
1990	22.0	101.3	85.2	16.1	272.6
1991	4.0	29.5	97.6	–68.1	204.5
1992	1.0	1.5	114.6	–113.1	91.4
1993	0.0	0.0	65.0	–65.0	26.4
1994	0.0	0.0	58.2	–58.2	–31.8

Loan activity centred in Australia, Canada and the United States, where most of the rapid growth in mine development took place during the 1980s. There are, however, outstanding loans also in Indonesia, Papua New Guinea, Brazil, Chile, Spain and New Zealand.

---

[5] *Gold 1988*, Consolidated Gold Fields Gold Survey, London 1989

[6] Jacks, Jessica, 'Forwards, Spot Deferreds, Options and Gold Loans', June 1991, and 'Forwards, Spot Deferreds, Options and Gold Loans – An Update', April 1992, both in *Nikkei Research Institute of Industry and Markets Gold Report*, Tokyo

The size of the individual loans depends on the structure of the local mining industry. In Australia, gold production registered a nine-fold increase between 1980 and 1988[7]. This was made up by numerous new mines each producing on average only 0.5–2 tonnes of gold annually. So the gold loan industry in Australia is characterised by at least 70 transactions, each averaging no more than 44,000 ounces (1.4 tonnes). During the same period, Canadian output increased 2.5 times. Fewer gold loans were drawn down although they tended to be larger, each averaging almost 70,000 ounces (2.2 tonnes).

In the United States, where gold output rose ten-fold, loans were usually similar to those in Canada. However, small loans of under 1 tonne appear to have been drawn down in the earlier years; the larger loans of anything between 100,000 and 300,000 ounces (3–9 tonnes) came mainly in 1987 and 1988. But any assessment of what is typical of the gold loan industry in the United States must exclude two large loans: Newmont Mining raised a loan of 1 million ounces (31.1 tonnes) and American Barrick secured a loan with the facility to draw down 1.05 million ounces. (American Barrick subsequently elected not to draw down the full amount and this has been taken into account in the summary table.) These two loans were exceptional in size and therefore would greatly distort the US average.

The cost of drawing down a gold loan during the peak of borrowing activity ranged from around 0.5–3% per annum, making this form of financing particularly attractive compared with the cost of borrowing money. Gold borrowing costs are a function of the cost of borrowing money, less the interest rate difference between spot and forward gold prices. Historically, the central banks lending gold achieved a return of 0.25–0.75% per annum. The earlier gold loans were drawn down at a fixed interest rate. As the structure of the loans became more sophisticated, the later agreements included a variable rate of interest often based on the London bullion market rate as quoted by Reuters.

An analysis of the data shows that the average weighted price achieved for the known gold loans was $420 per ounce, although some companies secured far higher prices. This implies that the value of all loans still outstanding in 1990, when the cumulative total was highest, was $3.4 billion.

The mining industry's short to medium-term view on price influences

---

[7] *Gold 1988*, Consolidated Gold Fields Gold Survey, London 1989

the rate at which gold loans are negotiated. A gold loan is essentially a forward sale, in that the mining company locks in a specific price for a substantial proportion of planned production. Mining companies will sell forward if they believe that the price is likely to weaken. This was particularly the case in Australia throughout the late 1980s and early 1990s, where producers were not only concerned about the US dollar gold price but also the price in their local currency. If miners believe that gold prices are likely to increase, they will be less prepared to incur the opportunity cost associated with locking in a price that may be lower than the spot price. A similar rationale applies to gold loans.

When prices were testing the $425–$430 per ounce range in early 1990, mining companies were committed to selling forward for hedging purposes and consequently new gold loans were being negotiated at that price. Thereafter, the price declined for three years. This bearish trend, combined with the lower cost of borrowing US dollars, has made gold loans an increasingly less attractive alternative. Moreover, substantially fewer new projects or expansions were given the go-ahead and less capital was required.

Gold loans on the whole have been very successful with relatively few failures[8]. There have been five known defaults, but the amount of gold associated with them is insignificant compared to the tonnage of loans completed and those that have already been paid back. Draw downs associated with these defaults were only 198,000 ounces (6.2 tonnes), compared to the overall cumulative total of over 610 tonnes and known paybacks in excess of 300 tonnes. Only 2% of the current outstanding industry is in default, which compares favourably with any currency denominated loan industry. This is especially true in the light of price declines during 1988 and 1989 which rendered the unhedged proportion of the primary industry less and less profitable.

An analysis of the **cost curve** and the overall level of hedging currently in place suggests that the industry is likely to maintain this good track record. The capacity at the top end of the cost curve comprises a number of South African mines that have been in operation for many years and were not funded through gold loans. Gold loan defaults, however, are not solely a function of the overall profitability of gold mining. A cost analysis cannot take adequate account of projects that may default for reasons specific to the mines themselves such as mining or milling problems or the

[8] Jacks, Jessica, 'The Gold Loan Industry', *Financial Times*, London, 14 February 1990

failure to achieve the necessary head grades. While there may be isolated incidents of mine failure in future, possibly in Canada or Australia, the amount of gold involved in a loan default will be small. Therefore there is little chance of a gold loan failure causing a price squeeze in the physical market as a mining company attempts to cover loan repayments that it cannot meet from its own production.

While most of the draw downs were seen in 1988, it is unlikely that the gold loan was merely a passing phase; indeed it has already become a permanent feature of the gold market. As with all derivatives, the nature and structure of bullion financing is expected to evolve in response to changing financial and economic variables, many of which are outside to the gold market itself. Furthermore, gold loans in future years will continue to reflect the structure of the underlying mining industry and its view on price trends.

Paybacks are now well under way. With the notable exception of Newmont Mining, which closed out the balance of its 1 million ounce loan in early 1992, there has been very little in the way of early repayments. The fact that most other mining companies have not followed suit has been rather surprising. Originally it seemed that this has not occurred because of the capital gains tax accrued in closing out a loan at a lower spot price than it was originally secured. Another reason could have been the cost of refinancing associated with an early payback. However, it appears that there are some genuine accounting problems associated with the early redemption of a gold loan, particularly in North America. The capital gain associated with the early payback has to be deferred and therefore does not gain immediate recognition in the current company accounts[9].

In future, the type of loan agreed on is likely to become more sophisticated and innovative as the industry begins to make maximum use of the flexible financial instruments available to it. For example, it seems reasonable to assume that the market will see more conversions from currency denominated loans to bullion loans and vice versa in what has become termed **multiple-option financing**. These agreements allow the borrower to renegotiate, usually on an annual basis, whether interest and capital repayments are made in gold or hard currency.

The use of gold loans need not be limited to mining companies only.

[9] Cameron, D., Dent, B., Pearman, R., *Mining: Accounting for Gold Loans and Forward Sales*, pp1-8, Ernst & Young, Toronto, 1989

Refiners, for example, have made use of this means of raising capital. The gold loan drawn down by Goldcorp in Australia was used to finance the Perth Mint's refinery and bullion coin division.

Another factor that is likely to have an influence on gold loans stems from the lending sources, specifically the central banks. Central banks did receive a rude shock in the Drexel, Burnham, Lambert collapse (discussed in chapter 5) in 1990. Their immediate reaction was one of caution, sharp retraction and a reluctance to continue lending to American security houses. This placed severe upward pressure on the cost of borrowing gold. Since this initial hesitation the central banks gradually relaxed their lending policies and the gold lease rates showed the corresponding decline. But any similar crisis in future could curtail the supply of gold for loans.

How do gold loans influence the spot price?

Some market participants claimed originally, at some length, that gold loans did not impact on the physical market and hence did not influence the price. They argued that gold loans do not represent accelerated supplies to the market, rather they were merely stock changes and it was suggested that including them in a supply/demand balance led to double counting[10]. A spokesman for one of the lending banks has also claimed that gold loans have been unjustly blamed for dips in the gold price[11]. With more experience, however, the market generally agrees that gold loans not only influence the short-term physical market and hence the price, but also have a negative, and sometimes very irrational, influence on short-term market sentiment.

New gold loan draw downs were frequently reported in the daily press and monthly mining journals, not to mention company reports. If the market sentiment at the time was negative, these loans were then immediately cited as a reason why the price was weak. In many cases, however, the loan was simply a delivery against a forward commitment entered into weeks previously and therefore had already been discounted in the price

---

[10] Christian, Jeffrey, 'Why Gold Loans are not Important to You and Me', CPM Group Precious Metals Quarterly Report, Gold, pp19-25, New York, 1989
[11] Newport, Don, 'Gold Loans: Recent Developments', paper to the Institute of Mining and Metallurgy Finance Conference, London, October 1990

weeks if not months earlier. It is interesting to note that, with the exception of the Newmont loan, there is usually no mention of the paybacks that are currently under way. This could be construed as being, at the least, supportive of or even positive for the short-term price. The lack of reporting is understandable since the paybacks are gradual, usually on a monthly or quarterly basis, whereas the loan draw downs are 'one-off' events which lend themselves to media coverage. To achieve a balanced view of the market therefore, an analysis of company accounts and preferably **10K-reports** is warranted and account should be taken of both the loan draw downs and the paybacks. In 1992 alone paybacks amounted to almost 115 tonnes (3.7 million ounces), quite a significant factor on the demand side of the equation. And in 1993 and 1994 it was close to 60 tonnes.

Finally, what happens when the gold loan is repaid? In theory, an agreed proportion (depending on the size of the loan) of the gold produced from a gold loan-funded project has already been sold and should be delivered back to the original lending bank, instead of coming onto the market. Therefore, while the short-term impact of the original loan on the price is clearly negative, the longer-term outcome, in theory, ought to be positive. In practice, however, this is probably not entirely the case. While the loan draw downs are usually completed in a single transaction over a matter of days or weeks, the paybacks occur gradually over a number of years. As I have indicated, the culmulative payback in some years has been substantial, but even then it is more of a daily trickle. Therefore, the beneficial impact on the price, even under normal circumstances, is likely to be less pronounced than the original negative impact. Furthermore, in some cases, the loans are rolled over and hence the positive impact is constantly being diluted.

7

WHO USES DERIVATIVES?

In theory any one participating in today's gold market could find a derivative product or a suite of products which could either assist with risk management or enhance profit potential. This is what the products were designed to do. But interestingly, while some market sectors instantly took to derivatives, and now probably could not operate efficiently without them, others have been reluctant even to take that first step. In practice the committed users are principally the bullion dealers themselves, along with many mining companies, several central banks, investors using warrants and, most recently, funds.

Over the years, I have counted the growing number of followers and, more importantly, their increasing commitment to different products. The transformation that has occurred was something that many thought impossible. Over time, certain derivative users have emerged and dominated for a while before stepping out of the limelight and making way for another end user. Each has had a turn in taking centre stage and enjoying their moment of preeminence. This ebb and flow of end users is simply a function of market circumstances at the time. No doubt this process will continue, but to attempt to forecast future trends as to who will dominate as an end user and when this will happen is virtually impossible.

After completing my initial work on producer hedging, I was actually concerned about running out of a fruitful research topic. It seemed then that I had covered all I could in terms of gold derivatives. Happily, my worries were not only unfounded but also short lived since a matter of months later the central banks made their cumulative appearance as substantial call option grantors. After the official sector's foray into option writing, once again I sat back thinking: now what, if anything at all? Sure enough, it was not long before I had another sector to research. I confess that I had never heard of Commodity Trading Advisors, let alone appreciated that they would be the next sector to emerge as another end user of gold derivatives. Of course, at that stage, I had not yet even touched on the massive hedge funds.

THE BULLION DEALERS

I suspect that many people, except for the dealers themselves of course, overlook the importance of the bullion dealing community. This is a grave oversight since their importance is not only in terms of the volume of business that they transact but the fact that they have a foot firmly entrenched in two distinct camps. The dealers are not only the architects of most of the tailor-made products, often taken for granted by their customers, but they are also substantial users of the derivatives in their own right. Apart from dealing on behalf of their customers, they can and do have very large exposures associated with their own books; positions that require hedging on a regular basis. They normally delta hedge any option transaction that they have taken on in the same way as they have to hedge forward sales that they have executed on behalf of the producers. Apart from this, they could well establish their own positions in the market. The dealing community can be considered one of the constant factors in the derivative equation although their focus could change with time and circumstance.

Attempting to assess the nature and size of the dealing community's exposure to derivatives is like trying to complete a huge jigsaw puzzle, the picture of which is simply a blank piece of paper. However you try and fit the pieces together, nothing but a blank image emerges. Having come to terms with the disappointment that I will never even catch a glimpse of the real picture, I have come to appreciate that different bullion banks have very variable client bases. For example, some are particularly exposed to the producers and have indeed geared their products and marketing to the mining industry. Others may have a predominance of central bank business or the fabricating side of the market.

The whole situation is complicated further by the fact that the nature and make-up of a bullion bank's trading book can and does change with time. This stands to reason, of course, as the presence of, and level of activity generated by, their clients waxes and wanes with time and market conditions. In 1990, for example, a trading book may have shown a bias towards the producers when market circumstances first encouraged a wave of hedging. Two years later, this same book may have exhibited less producer hedging but more central banks options. By 1994, the funds were dominant and the central bank options were almost a memory of days gone by. Who knows what tomorrow may bring? Possibly a resurgence of producer business, a return of the official sector or even the emergence of a new end user.

THE MINING COMPANIES

If the dealers paved the way, the mining industry has played a key role in the way in which the gold derivative market has evolved. The miners responded to a number of factors that fortuitously came together during the 1980s. The mining booms in Australia and North America as a result of the price rallies in 1979 and 1980 and the advent of cheap heap leach technology meant that the industry was expanding rapidly and well placed to accept mining finance and later risk management instruments. High interest rates, which made borrowing metal more attractive than borrowing dollars, encouraged a wave of **gold loan** activity as producers scrambled to raise the capital necessary to take their projects off the drawing boards and bring them to fruition. High interest rates, however, also implied a healthy **contango** waiting to be earned via the increasingly liquid forward market. Then on Black Monday, in October 1987, equity markets around the world collapsed, making it even more attractive for the miners to execute a gold loan rather than run the risk of relying on equity financing.

The derivative pioneers in the mining community were the Australians. The numerous mining companies there had senior staff with the financial experience who fully understood derivative products and their applications. I was amazed to meet with one group of Australian mining executives, who rather proudly told me that they were not miners at all! The board of directors of this company did not have one geologist, mining engineer or metallurgist among them. They all had financial back-grounds and a fair percentage were ex-foreign exchange dealers. Small wonder they took the attitude: 'We do not produce metal for jewellery fabrication. We produce currency and we monetise it before it comes out of the ground.' So the Australians got on with the job of monetising their output, especially ahead of a profits tax that was imposed in 1991.

North American miners were quick to follow suit, even without the incentive of selling ahead of a new tax. As US production rose ten-fold in scarcely a decade, and Canadian output tripled, their overall level of hedging soon represented a significant percent of total annual output. This led to the inevitable debate as to whether or not the mining industry was over-hedged. This concern led me to ask the mining companies directly. In a global survey, I put various questions to them, relating to how they viewed hedging. The two following charts show the overall results of my survey which covered the three years 1990 to 1992 inclusive.

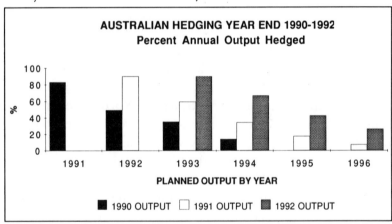

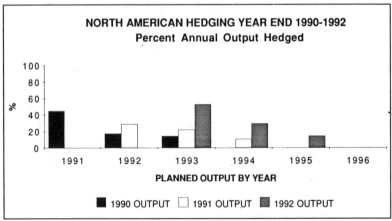

Compare the two and it is obvious that the Australians initially were more hedged than the North Americans, who later began to catch up. It also shows that the Australians were happy selling a higher percent of their production further out than their American counterparts. I also found changes in product preferences both geographically and chronologically.

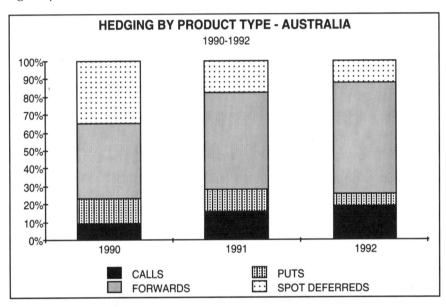

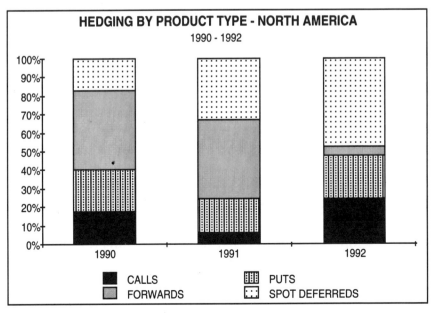

Over the three year period, the Australians made increasing use of the forward contract at the expense of the spot deferred. This was probably a function of interest rates. Throughout this period the miners also appeared comfortable with entering into min-max strategies, whereby they secured price protection by buying put options but incurred less or no costs in doing this through the granting of calls options. By 1992, some of the mining companies were simply granting call options and viewing the premium as a means of enhancing their revenue streams.

In contrast, in 1991 the North Americans appeared less happy with the buying put/granting calls programmes although they returned to options in 1992. Furthermore, they virtually deserted the forward sale in favour of the spot deferred contract. Again, this was probably a function of local interest rates, which at times moved in opposite directions to those in Australia.

Some mining companies were happy to lock in excess of 100% of a year's planned production (possible through options and spot deferred contracts), but I noted with interest that the majority rated their percentage already hedged and their planned output as the primary determinants of decision making. To my surprise, the US dollar price and the local price of gold ranked only third. Also high on the list of priorities were the views of the companies' boards, the companies' cost structure, the perception of their shareholders and the mines' reserve bases.

The potential loss of upside participation in a higher spot price appeared to be of less concern since this worry is the domain of those companies still to embark on a hedging programme. They were also less concerned about limitations to existing credit lines and the lease rate.

I asked the producers whether or not they were comfortable with their overall level of hedging. The majority of mining companies said they were prepared to buy back their forwards, although most had not considered that they were overhedged. The 1993 price rally provided the market with a good testing time and I waited to see if indeed the mining companies would unwind their hedges. There were some who liquidated their exposures, but the majority allowed their programmes to run their full course. This bears out my claim in 1993 that the gold price needed to average (not just rally briefly) to over $420/oz before the producers felt pressurised enough to prune their hedges[1].

[1] Jacks, Jessica, 'New Strategies in the Derivative Business', paper presented at the Financial Times Gold Conference, Istanbul, June 1993

Within the mining community, there are a number of derivative-related concerns that are voiced regularly. The most emotive question is whether we should be hedging in the first place, a theme I address later (chapter 8). However, there are other worries that go beyond this. Many of the producers have acknowledged that they do not have the facilities to cross-check the fairness of the pricing and do not fully understand the principles behind many of the more complex derivatives. Others expressed a difficulty in getting their senior management to understand more complex hedging. There is a communication problem, which I address later in this chapter. Suffice to say now that the bullion bankers could assist by ensuring that they bring a language that everybody around the table can understand into a meeting between themselves and the mining industry.

THE CENTRAL BANKERS

For a very brief, but intensive, period in 1992 and early 1993 the market saw the emergence of the central banks as option grantors. Writing out-of-the-money calls earns a premium for them and renders their gold reserves interest bearing. The premium appears to have been the sole motive for such a policy. But this activity raised a number of market and price-related questions which I put to the bullion dealing community. My survey came up with the following:

Firstly, in 1993, there were between 10 and 20 central banks actively granting options. They were primarily the central banks of the gold producing countries and from Latin America. There was also market participation, albeit more limited, from the Middle East, Pacific Rim and the Far East. Interestingly, the dealers reported no option activity from Europe, specifically the G7 countries, and only a little from the CIS. There was also very little correlation between those central banks who wrote options and those who were actively lending gold into the market.

Reliable figures on the level of outstanding central bank calls at the peak of this activity in early 1993 are hard to ascertain. However, a total of around 15 million ounces or 466 tonnes was widely accepted by the market. My survey indicated that they tended to be written between 5–10% out of the money and that they appeared to be relatively short lived, perhaps out to three months. Given this relatively limited life, it is virtually impossible to estimate the net year-on-year primary or secondary delta hedging that may have been associated with these exposures. But hedging against them certainly existed.

Then, in mid-1993, the unthinkable happened. The gold price increased to the extent that these calls came into the money. I suspect that many of them were exercised against the central banks. It appears as though the banks simply delivered metal against their exposures because, without exception, all those bullion dealers responding to my question-naire four months earlier, maintained that the central banks were not concerned about being 'called away'. They commented that the central banks had consciously granted calls at **strike prices** at which they were happy to deliver gold. Once these options were exercised, have we seen the official sector re-establishing their options? The answer is probably no, or certainly not in nearly the same volume as previously seen. But this does not necessarily imply that the central banks have withdrawn from the option market permanently. Time and changes in market circumstance could well bring them back into the fray.

THE FUNDS

The 1993 price rise brought another end user into the market in the form of the fund manager, based mainly in the United States – not a newcomer but someone who was absent from the market for more than a decade. This return was highly significant because ten years ago the fund manager did not have access to the vast array of derivatives available today. My research into this sector is in its infancy, but in relation to derivatives, some signals are emerging.

There are two specific types of funds that are currently involved with gold; the large hedge funds and the so-called Commodity Trading Advisors or CTAs. I appreciate that there are many other categories and definitions of funds, but for my purposes this initial division suffices. The reason for my differentiation is that I suspect that the hedge funds make use of the OTC derivative market and the CTAs use the exchange products. Their potential influence could therefore differ in more ways than simply in the magnitude of their activities.

As far as the massive hedge funds are concerned, I would be very surprised to hear that a fund, like Quantum or Mint, would take a large futures or options position on COMEX or any other exchange. The whole transaction would just be too transparent and the entire market would know about it within hours of it being executed. This would be equivalent to one of the largest mining houses hedging a good deal of its production directly via the COMEX floor and we know that this sort of activity is generally not done. Thus we can deduce that the OTC market enjoyed the fruits of the famous forays by George Soros' Quantum Fund and Sir James Goldsmith, the Ango-French entrepreneur, into the gold market in mid-1993. However since these OTC transactions were in turn hedged by the various counter parties, some of this business could have been offset on the exchange. The relationship between the exchanges and the huge hedge funds is therefore an indirect one.

Now why should the CTAs be any different? I have found a number of good reasons. Firstly, they are very small compared with the hedge funds. I monitor almost 400 of them and cumulatively they control $11 billion dollars; substantially less than the money managed by one of the large hedge funds. This implies that they do not have the financial muscle to secure the credit lines necessary to delve into the OTC derivative market. Secondly, they are primarily programme traders where discretionary override of their computer-generated buy and sell signals is limited perhaps to entry and exit points or to which market they should be dealing in. Programme trading based on technical analysis requires public domain information regarding the commodity concerned. The OTC market does not publish anything at all, but COMEX makes available data series such as open interest and turnover. This data can be charted and, together with a price series, can be technically assessed. Once this is done, the CTAs then tend to make use of the very product that they have analysed, namely the COMEX gold futures and options contracts.

There is one more important factor as regards the CTAs. These funds tend to be small, most having less than $5 million under management. They also require from their investors a remarkably low minimum account level, anything from $100,000 to $500,000. Very few insist on more than $1 million to begin trading on behalf of an investor. At face value this seems to imply that they are gearing their activities to high net worth individuals at the retail end of the business. While in general this is probably true, it is not necessarily always the case. A number of them are being allocated money from the large state pension funds, primarily in the United States, with which they are given discretionary mandates to trade commodities.

There is also evidence that the CTAs are receiving funds from some central banks, largely from Asia and the Pacific Rim. To date, there is no evidence to suggest that the CTAs are trading gold on behalf of the central banks, but they are certainly trading currencies. This broader source of funding being channelled into the CTAs, over and above private clients, may have bearing on the gold market in the future.

Will the funds always be interested in gold? The answer is allied to interest rate movements. When interest rates are low, gold becomes more competitive compared to other investment alternatives. When interest rates rise, gold's attraction soon fades. In short the funds re-assess their portfolio allocations as interest rates shift.

AND WHO NEXT?

Perhaps fabricators of jewellery or industrial products will finally enter the market in a way other than being substantial borrowers of gold. So far, however, they have shown little interest for several reasons.

The first is historical. The well established European fabricators are often old family businesses, set in their ways with a traditional approach to management. When I visited some of them for the Consolidated Gold Fields Gold Survey, I was struck at the owners' reluctance to consider buying gold forward in a rising market. Needless to say, we never got around to discussing buying a call option.

Secondly, many are small family-run concerns which lack the financial resources to secure the credit lines necessary for a hedging programme, even if they were interested.

The third reason for their reluctance relates to price. Gold derivatives have really emerged since 1980, while the gold price has usually been declining. Lower prices favoured the jewellery fabricators which eliminated the very need for them to consider hedging in the first place.

The final reason for fabricator reluctance relates to taxation. In some countries jewellery is often fabricated from undeclared metal, smuggled across boarders to avoid taxes, duties and surcharges. A large visible hedging programme might therefore attract unwanted attention to the real, as opposed to the declared, level of business completed by the fabricator.

EDUCATING THE CLIENT

Whoever is the predominant end user at any given moment, the derivative revolution has changed not only the character of trading desks around the world, but also the dealer-client relationship. The introduction of complex products into the mainstream of day-to-day business has required any bank competing seriously in derivatives to hire highly educated graduates with degrees, if not doctorates, in applied mathematics, advanced statistics and often physics and engineering. They are the only people qualified to deal with the pricing and risk assessment of the more advanced derivatives. While banks must rely on this intellectual input, they must not lose sight of the practicalities of running a business, nor of being able to explain the mysteries of derivatives to clients who may well lack such advanced qualifications. The wizard trader may understand the mathematics, but lack the pragmatism and commercial experience to make it comprehendable and attractive to customers. Indeed, the more esoteric the intellectual thinking, the more the creators of derivatives are distanced from the eventual users.

Banks, therefore, must maintain a balanced mix of personality and expertise within their derivative teams. I cannot emphasise this too strongly. No matter how innovative or exciting a product may be, if it cannot be marketed in a meaningful, user-friendly way, the derivative may never see the light of day. The successful marketing of a derivative lies not so much with the technicalities of the product itself, but rather in the public relations skills and communication skills that go with its launch. Having spent my entire working career within the mining industry, I have sat through many, often painful and embarrassing, presentations where a bullion bank attempts either to convince a mining company that it should hedge or attempts to sell to an already committed hedger a particular package. Unfortunately, all too often, the meeting is more than just a complete failure and can actually damage the client-bank relationship. This is not a problem confined only to mining companies. Central banks have sometimes been just as dazed.

The trouble is that the bank may do an outstanding job developing the product, but fail to gear the presentation to the audience. Without a thorough appreciation of how well the audience understands the gold market and the associated derivatives, the banks, completely unwittingly, can either insult the intelligence of the audience by talking down to them or alienate them by talking straight over their heads and totally confusing them. Either way, the banks must then expect a guarded response. A senior central banker or mining executive does not take kindly to a 28 year old trader, no matter how bright and enthusiastic, bouncing into his office for thirty minutes and telling him how to make risk-free money out of his reserves, whether these reserves are in the bank vaults or in the ground. You cannot blame the client for asking: where's the catch? These managers are also going to feel equally uncomfortable facing someone who launches into the intricacies of the delta, gamma, theta and vega of a particular outlandish option.

In my opinion, banks should spend almost as much time perfecting their presentation skills as they do generating the products in the first place. The most successful presentations that I have seen are done by a senior executive of a bullion bank, similar in age to his central bank or mining counterpart. His knowledge of the derivatives may indeed be slightly superficial compared with the creator of the option, and he may not have sat on a dealing desk for many years, but he can answer basic questions about a full range of derivative strategies. His advantage is that he understands the mining and central banking communities. Even dress and body language have a remarkable effect on the potential client. A man in his late forties or early fifties, with the calm voice that carries with it the tone of years of experience, is like a tonic for the stressed mining executive. This bullion banker in a conservative navy-blue suit, cream shirt and understated tie (no bright red braces or cellular telephone) will have an immediate calming effect. Once the mining executive no longer feels threatened, half the battle is won.

A successful client-bank relationship does not end there. Central bankers or miners expect a long-term relationship, where trust is not built up overnight or by one-off thirty minute presentations. They want continuity. Nothing unsettles a client more than a continual turnover in either bank customer relations officers or staff on the trading desks.

When a mining company is new to hedging, a bank should invest emotional and intellectual time and energy in the fledgling relationship. This requires working intensively with the miners until they feel comfortable with the strategy they finally adopt. A positive proposal for the nervous newcomer to derivatives is to encourage him to conduct a dummy run. Allow the company to establish theoretical credit lines and then hedge, in theory, a proportion of the production, on paper only, for a period of, say, three to six months. This involves indicating the costs incurred, the paper work involved and the choices of strategies. When I was learning I found it useful to run two or three different strategies concurrently, so I could experience for myself the differences between selling forward, buying put options or executing a min-max. During the trial run the banks can help the hedgers to unwind their positions and take 'profit' or allow them to incur some loss of upside potential. Thus, when the time comes for the real thing, they have had a taste of what it is all about. Experience has taught me that this will prove more fruitful than going to see the potential client and saying: 'with the knowledge of hindsight, you could have hedged at X price and the price is now Y'. We all know what we should have done 12 months ago. What we do not know is what we should be doing now. This concept of a dummy run has the added advantage of establishing trust and a two-way relationship which helps both sides immensely when the time comes for the mining company to negotiate the real credit lines.

The idea of a dummy run need not be limited to the novice hedger. It can equally effectively be applied to new products, especially some of the more exotic options. Why not let an experienced hedger 'test drive' your new product? An exotic option in this sense is no different than a new model of motor car and no one would dream of buying a new car before taking it out on the road for a spin.

8

THE GREAT HEDGING DEBATE

The question of whether or not producer hedging is a good thing has become one of the most hotly debated and emotive issues in the gold market; perhaps second only to whether or not central banks should indeed hold gold.

Over the years, as I learnt more about producer selling policies and watched the performance of the gold price under the weight of producer hedging, my own personal views have come around full circle.

At first, I was very enthusiastic indeed and probably for the right reasons. Working for a mining company, I assessed the hedging question strictly from a producer's viewpoint. Consequently, I placed the need to protect the company's balance sheet above all other criteria. The opportunity to remove one of the unknown variables, namely price risk, from our financial equation was most appealing. Then, in the late 1980s, I watched the cumulative volume of hedging clearly starting to cap the gold price, certainly in the short term. I began to ask myself some questions. Are the mining companies, by hedging a relatively small percentage of their production at higher prices, killing the goose that lays the proverbial golden egg? Are they jeopardising their long-term future by enhancing short-term gains? Was the decision to hedge correctly addressing the long-term aims of the gold mining industry?

I believe that these questions were justifiably asked, given the condition and the structure of the market prevailing at the time. It was a market characterised by prolonged, gradual, but almost unrelenting, downward pressure on the gold price. Many markets participants, dealers, fabricators and mining companies alike, will understand exactly what I am describing. It was a time when we were all attempting to keep our heads above water in very trying circumstances.

With hindsight, the impact that hedging had on the price, while very real, was probably exaggerated because of the overall market mood. During the late 1980s and early 1990s, a particular market sector was conspicuous in its absence. I am referring, of course, to the sophisticated investor in Europe and North America. In my opinion, this absence was merely a function of interest rates. While yields on government paper, bonds and even cash were substantially higher than the traditionally non-interest bearing assets, gold simply could not compete as a serious investment alternative. Without money under management and portfolio managers actively investing in gold, the supply/demand balance then came to rely more on the physical sectors of the market. The demand side of the equation had to be supported primarily by the price sensitive high carat jewellery offtake and bar hoarding in the Middle East, Far East, and the Indian sub-continent. In other words, the demand side would have done well without the added weight of the accelerated supplies that producer hedging exerted on the market. If there had been some investment interest emanating from Europe and North America, I am sure the impact that hedging had on the market would have been greatly ameliorated and perhaps would not have attracted the attention it did.

Market developments and the resultant behaviour of the price during 1994 demonstrated this to me very clearly. As interest rates came down, the commodities suddenly regained, if not all, certainly part of their competitiveness, and the way in which the funds returned to gold was well covered by the media. What I found most telling was the level of delta hedge buying against the wave of gold warrants that suddenly emerged. We do not know exactly the tonnage involved but it suffices to say that the level of buying was very substantial indeed. It instantly dwarfed the tonnages previously associated with a good deal of cumulative producer hedging completed during the preceding eighteen months. However, no one complained about the impact that this buying had on the market. It was merely another example of the derivatives in action but because everybody wanted a higher gold price no one spoke out against it.

I believe now that mining companies should hedge. After all, mining, whether it is for gold or antimony, is a competitive business and the individual companies should make use of all means available to them to enhance their competitive advantage. No one bats an eyelid or comments when a mine goes to great lengths to pare its operating costs in order to achieve that prestigious position in the lowest quartile of the global **cost curve**. That is what management is there for and paid to achieve. The same argument applies to a mine protecting its balance sheet. Mine management is answerable to its shareholders and the shareholders aim to invest in an efficiently run and well managed company which is going to declare a healthy dividend. It makes no difference whether the dividend comes from careful cost control, efficient mining and milling methods or active financial engineering. In fact, the ideal investment is in a stock whose management has the skills to manage all the areas of risk.

I have come to realise that we should not judge the individual or cumulative activities of any market participants. Market activity should not be interpreted as either a 'good' or a 'bad' thing, regardless of its impact on the gold price – but merely a fact of life. There is no escaping the fact that transactions are executed in the market and they all, to a greater or lesser degree, influence the gold price. We should monitor them and accept them as an integral part of the market, for better or for worse.

If, in the short term, what may benefit an individual company does not necessarily augur well for the market as a whole, then so be it. On occasions, producer hedging will not only influence the price, but may even act as the major price determinant. However, no sector can dominate the market indefinitely and the time will come when other players will move to centre stage and again have their day. These other members of the cast, by participating in the gold market theatre, may exert upward or downward pressure on the price. This influence on the price may come from physical transactions or the knock-on effect from the myriad of derivatives now available. Whatever the outcome, it will be a development to which we all will have to acclimatise and something we will have to accept, whether we as individuals choose to stand in judgement or not.

Having said all this, the hedging controversy continues and I am astonished at how impassioned the debate can become. There are still a number of anti-hedging arguments to which mining companies return over and over again, many with monotonous regularity. Some of these concerns may be valid under certain circumstances but, in general, most are not. A number of the concerns expressed demonstrate a lack of understanding of derivatives and their full scope and potential. I am in no way concluding that the derivatives are heaven sent cure-alls; I am very wary of many of the products and the way they are priced and marketed. However, mining companies should make every effort to understand the products before deciding whether or not a hedging programme is compatible with the company's corporate culture.

WHAT ARE THE ARGUMENTS AGAINST HEDGING?

The first concern about hedging is: **If a company sells forward, there is a potential loss of upside participation if the spot price shows a sustained rise over the forward price to which the company is committed.**

Yes, loss of upside does occur if the company makes very extensive and exclusive use of the forward market and then if the gold price averages (not just spikes) higher than the forward hedged price (which of course includes the **contango**). However, no one is advocating that a mining company should commit a large percentage of output to the forward market to the exclusion of other products or the spot price. The extent to which mine output should be hedged is a very subjective issue and I do not believe that any hard and fast rules can be applied across the industry. What may be ideal for one company or operation may be totally inappropriate for another. And this is the beauty of hedging – there is such a wide range of products available, offering enormous flexibility, that a hedging programme can be tailor-made to fit the exact requirements of an individual operation.

If I had to design a programme I would look closely at the mine's operating cost structure and its level of capital expenditure. I would also take into account the projected cost profile over the life of the mine. For example, is there any financial year during which capital replacement costs may be onerously high? The aim would be to answer the question: what price do we need to realise and secure a healthy (but not a greedy) consistent rate of return on our investment? Then I would calculate back how much output we would need to hedge, how far out and at what price? I would ask myself whether I felt intuitively comfortable with that figure.

I have always felt relaxed with the figure of 30% of current annual output committed to the programme. There is no logic or rationale behind this figure of mine, it simply feels right, but what may feel right for me may not suit someone else.

Now, if I did my calculation and discovered that at today's gold price, we needed to hedge 75% of current output to achieve our intended return, the figure might not bother me (although I might question the wisdom of opening this particular mine in the first place!). I certainly would not implement this level of hedging. I would, however, look for alternatives. For example, depending on the contango, I would look to the possibility of hedging less production but, crucially, for a longer period; in other words, making the most of compounding the contango year-on-year. Alternatively, I would structure an option strategy to augment a more conservative forward programme. Depending on the contango, I may decide not to sell forward at all, but attempt to achieve my goal through the use of options only. My point here is that, for a mining company, the hedging world is your oyster and it is up to you as the designer of a hedge programme to be creative and to make an effort to understand the products at your disposal in order to make the most of the flexibility offered by derivatives.

Taking the above discussion a little further, the bullion dealing community, in fact, has already responded efficiently to the mining companies' concern about potential loss of upside. The very successful launch of the **spot deferred** contract, for example, was no co-incidence, nor is the growing recognition that options are a very viable alternative.

Ultimately, the mining companies have to decide how serious this potential (but remember, not guaranteed) loss of upside participation is. If we have committed 30% of output at a price of $350/oz and the gold price actually moves higher throughout the life of the forward contract, I maintain that the opportunity cost associated with 30% of our output will be more than offset by the windfall profits made on the remaining 70% of production which we will be selling into the spot market. Surely, this is a very acceptable price to pay for that down side protection and insurance which may tide the mine over some very lean times when the gold price may be behaving like a vindictive child?

The companies need to ask themselves which is more important, hedging a proportion of production which effectively covers costs and ensures the survival of an operation or the opportunity cost of not being able to sell all one's output at a higher price? Bear in mind that higher prices are what miners dream about – they are not guaranteed. However, operating costs, capital expenditure and interest charges are not fantasy or a pipe dream; they are a very real threat when it comes to mine closures, financial losses and labour redundancies.

The next anti-hedging argument is: **Oh yes, options may allow participation in price rallies, but they are expensive and over-priced.**

I agree that there is no such thing as a free lunch and companies must pay for what they want. Consequently, the industry must expect to pay a price for the flexibility of the option. I also agree that options can be expensive, but this does not necessarily imply that they are over-priced. The cost of the option depends on the type of option and how near to the money it is at the time of purchase. Options that are close to being in the money will be expensive, anything up to $10–15 per ounce or more. Out-of-the-money options can cost less than $0.50 per ounce.

The company must decide where they want their option **strike price** relative to the spot price of gold at the time. If they are particularly risk averse and want options near to the money, they must not complain if they are expensive!

It is also important to bear in mind that the cost of protective options can be offset completely or in part by granting limited and conservative options. In other words, the premium that is earned for writing options pays for the price protection. But, again, nothing comes for nothing and by reducing these costs, we should expect some potential loss of upside participation via the options granted. If carefully designed, however, this loss of upside will be only a small fraction of total production and significantly less than selling forward.

Many mining companies are currently viewing the cost of limited price protection, via options, as a very acceptable addition to operating costs. I believe that this is the correct, pragmatic approach. They regard the price of the option as an insurance premium. If they insure plant equipment and are happy to pay an annual premium for this insurance, why not insure the gold price?

This then brings me to the producers' concerns about over pricing. The answer is simply this: if you think that your option quote is over priced, shop around a little and get a number of quotes as you would when shopping for golf clubs or a motor car. There is no difference. Competition in the option market is cut throat and dealers are anxious to give very competitive quotes. Option dealers guilty of loading their option premia simply will not win the tender.

On this issue, there is one further point of relevance. When asking for a price quote on options, make a habit of asking the dealer about the implied volatility used when pricing the option. This implied volatility is the only subjective variable used when pricing an option and this is where dealers will diverge in their views. Nine times out of ten, if you get two very different option quotes, you will find the answer lies in markedly dissimilar implied volatilities. Remember that the higher the implied volatility, the higher the price of the option. If dealers are using recent historical data to calculate their volatilities, then the smart miner buys options when the price has been stable for a while! Conversely, be cautious about buying options when the gold price has been bouncing around all over the place.

The third favourite anti-hedging argument is: **We hear everything you are saying about hedging, but only high cost mines need to hedge – our mines are low cost.**

To some extent, this is true, but I not do believe that enjoying a position in the lowest quartile of the cost curve justifies financial complacency at head office.

The higher the operating costs, the more urgent the need for some sort of price protection. But in a **contango** market, the opportunity cost incurred in not taking advantage of higher prices, even for low cost mines, can be very substantial.

Quite apart from this, low operating costs do not necessarily imply higher profitability. I once did a rather telling exercise. I gathered information on a number of mining companies and compared their operating costs with their realised, achievable prices. In other words, I assessed a mine's competitiveness in terms of revenue rather than costs. The results shot this anti-hedging argument down in flames. It showed that, because of extensive hedging by the majority of gold producers, enjoying a position in the lowest quartile of the cost curve no longer automatically implied that the operation was one of the most profitable. Low costs do not necessarily imply greater profitability relative to the high cost (but hedged) mine next door. The converse was also true. Some mines with very high operating costs were far from loss-making. Quite the contrary, and, thanks to hedging, they were well placed on the revenue curve.

While on the question of cost, I must have my say about the mining industry's preoccupation with being in the lowest quartile of the cost curve. This curve deals with operating or cash costs only. The financing and interest charges are not accounted for in these figures. There are many examples where acceptable operating costs are incurred but the financing charges are very high. This is commonly seen with newly commissioned mines before the capital expenditure has been amortized. In my mind, the need for price protection then becomes even more pressing.

Then of course comes the complaint: **Hedging is speculative!**

Whenever I come across this argument, I recall a meeting with a typical Australian producer some years back. He had obviously been faced with the same retort and his response was: 'Rubbish, it's the bloody mining side of our business that is speculative!'

He is, of course, correct. Cautiously selling 30% of output to remove some price exposure seems remarkably risk averse when compared with the challenge of committing millions of dollars into sinking a shaft or three, often in a politically unsettled country, coping with steep thermal gradients and possibly unstable geological anomalies, relying on good rock mechanics and metallurgical processes and being confident enough to promise that you will be able to recondition the environment back to its original state twenty years hence. Mining companies take all these physical and financial risks without being guaranteed that when they get to the working face, they will actually find the gold grades that they were hoping for in the first place!

I have always stressed that it is critical to differentiate between a speculative position entered into by an investor or trader with a very short time perspective and a long-term price protection plan entered into by a mining company. In terms of using the terminal markets, they are on opposing ends of the spectrum. Hedging should be seen as price protection and should be viewed as insurance against a volatile price, which has not been particularly kind to the mining industry in recent years and is not likely to change. This is my view and I know it differs to that of some mining companies which may be adopting a trading position. I would not advocate this and my attitude to a hedging programme is if it's not broken, don't fix it. Just let it run its natural course and over time it will serve you well.

Of course there are a number of often quoted hedging cases where 'something' went very wrong. It is unfortunate that, like one vacation marred by nasty weather or the one tainted bottle of wine from an otherwise excellent vinyard, the one hedging programme that fails is remembered long after all the profits associated with the successful programmes have been distributed in the form of dividends.

There are two reasons why a hedging programme can go wrong. The first is that the company uses derivatives products with which it is not sufficiently familiar. The second is when a, usually junior, staff member is given signing power to hedge and runs amok in the market. In both instances, I blame lack of management control for the trouble. In the first case, invest some money in hiring skilled staff and give them the software and latitude to master the derivatives. It will pay off handsomely. Get the right people on board and they will instinctively ask the right questions and do the right thing. The same applies to the second problem although I do believe that each hedging programme should be executed within broad but controlling parameters. There are a number of ways in which hedging can be kept on track without 'strait jacketing' either the programme or programmer. For example, board approval of a hedging programme may include one or a combination of the following provisos (and this list is by no means exhaustive):

- At any one time, no more than X% may be hedged via any product;
- At any one time, no more than X% of established credit lines with all bullion dealers may be tied to the hedging programme;
- Below a certain spot trigger price, the programme is put on hold and no new transactions may be executed;
- Options exceeding a cost of X cents per ounce are deemed to be too expensive and may not be purchased.

These tram lines give the treasurer involved plenty of leeway to run a flexible hedging programme without it getting out of control. This, together with weekly reporting to the board, should pre-empt any unwelcome and unilateral decisions on the part of the treasurer.

Perhaps bullion dealers can provide an early warning system. Dealers have certain credit lines and limits in place which are governed by mutually accepted agreements, entered into with the mining company. If the dealers suddenly receive orders from an individual in a company to execute deals that patently transgress the original agreement, the dealer should ring the alarm bells.

It is important to be realistic about hedging and accept that occasionally, the price protection programme is going to under perform relative to the spot price. When this happens, and it will, I have utmost respect for management who stand by their treasurer rather than scouting around, looking for someone to blame. This happens all too often. I have seen management turn a blind eye and tolerate a hedging programme while it is outperforming the spot price, but the moment there is any hint of potential opportunity costs, management turns against hedging and blames the person who executed the deals in the first place. The fact that the treasurer was probably only doing his job to the best of his ability seems to be deemed beside the point. The 'I told you so' accusations start and then things can become really acrimonious. Either management must sanction hedging and then live peacefully with the decision or it must never give authorisation for hedging in the first place. One or the other – management must not play it both ways depending on the profit/loss position at any one time.

Often I have noticed that when anti-hedgers are feeling as though they may be losing the hedging debate, they then pass the buck to the shareholder. **'Aha,' they say, 'the shareholders want the high risk/reward exposure of the gold price and if a company hedges, the very reason for investing in gold equity is undermined. Hedging, therefore, reflects a poor understanding on management's part of what the shareholder wants.'**

Well, what do shareholders want? To be perfectly candid, they probably want to have their cake, eat it too, and from what I have seen of AGMs, will not say no to a smoked salmon sandwich. Shareholders, quite justifiably, expect the company in which they have invested to be well managed. To this extent, they will probably expect down side protection against adverse metal prices. But they also want a decent rate of return on capital, which implies to me that, if this is achieved, they will be less likely to complain about the occasional and marginal loss of upside participation in the gold price. Ask shareholders what they would want least – to see their investments going to the wall, or being less gearing to an anticipated, but not guaranteed, rally in the gold price?

The next question is whether management actually takes the time to understand their shareholders. In my experience, the major shareholders of most mining companies are institutional investors, often pension funds and managers of unit trusts or the portfolios of high nett worth individuals. I understand the role of a pension fund manager to be the provider of steady, reliable returns to their aging dependents, in which case, a high risk/reward, commodity price driven, roller coaster is the very last thing the pension funds want. However, I do appreciate that the fund business is a very competitive one indeed. Attracting new funds depends very much on the portfolio manager's last quarterly results relative to his competitors. I have always felt that this brings an undesirably short-term perspective to what essentially should be a long-term business.

The next objection to hedging is what I believe to be a *non sequitur*. That is: **Management comes to rely on hedging and consequently they fail to pay adequate attention to cost cutting. Indirectly, through hedging, the mining operation therefore begins to creep up the cost curve.**

I do not see how cost cutting at mine level can have anything to do with hedging, which is normally done by head office, usually many miles away from the mine site. This is like claiming that if head office were to insure plant equipment, the mine personnel would be more likely to abuse that equipment. From what I can see, management is so preoccupied with remaining low cost, that it places continual pressure on staff at the mine to control outgoings, regardless of the hedge contracts in place. If I was a mine manager and constantly being nagged by head office about cost control, I would get rather irate if they were not hedging. I would believe that while I was keeping to my side of the bargain they were leaving me (and my miners) vulnerable in an area that ought to be firmly in control, namely price risk.

Not often, but at times, I have come across the hedging objection: **We are such a big producer that if we were to hedge, we will move the price.**

Any transaction in the market, no matter who completes it, can move the gold price. The important thing here is the depth and liquidity of the market at the time of the transaction. I have seen the gold market gobble up one million ounces of metal in a matter of seconds, lick its lips and then ask for more, without the price moving even 25 cents. I have also, however, seen the gold price shed more than a dollar when someone unwittingly tried to sell a mere fifty thousand ounces into a market already suffering from a bad bout of indigestion. What I am saying is, if the counter-party on the buy side is there, producer hedging will make very little difference to the immediate gold price. If the buyer is not there, the hedging, even from a tiny mine, will place pressure on the market. The skilled hedger knows when the market can take metal in volume or when to stay out of the market for a while.

The final objection to hedging was the one that floored me for the longest time. This was: **We are not purely a gold play. We have a diverse portfolio of commodities which provides us with a natural hedge. When the price of one commodity is down, we can rely on a counter-cyclical part of our portfolio to out perform the rest and therefore compensate for any losses. In other words, we are a natural hedge and therefore we do not need to make use of any these paper products.**

Let me counter argue this with an analogy from the agricultural sector. It is the same as a farmer who decides to farm tomatoes, for example. He elects not to plant a drought resistant variety because they tend to give a lower yield. Fine, but then he also elects not to irrigate his crop because water is expensive and so he relies on the elements for his rainfall. He recognises this and decides that, in case of drought, he cannot rely too much on the tomato crop for his living, so he also plants potatoes. Now, because of the totally unnecessary cost associated with buying pesticides, he decides not to spray the potato crop. But since he cannot be guaranteed that the potatoes will escape the dreaded potato blight, he decides that he also had better plant carrots. Now, carrots need a particular soil to flourish, otherwise the crop yield is rather mediocre. But this means that the farmer needs to spend more money on mineral additives…well, why bother with that expense because if the carrots fail, he still has his tomatoes and his potatoes.

Now, knowing this farmer's propensity to throw his lot in with fate, would you, as a sophisticated investor, dash off and queue for a prospectus if you heard that he was privatising?

Terminating a Contract

9

THE PROSPECT FOR DERIVATIVES: IS REGULATION ON THE WAY?

Derivatives are now an integral part of the gold market, just as they are in all financial and commodity trading. The evolution of a market to a progressively more sophisticated level appears, also, to be irrevocable. Markets apparently will not return to the steadier state that once prevailed. I used to be optimistic about the future of derivatives, but unsettling developments have made me less sanguine. Consequently, I approach the outlook for derivatives with some caution. In short, I remain a strong protagonist of the products; it is the manner in which they are now being used that I must now question.

Derivatives are in the process of undergoing a gruelling test of endurance during which market makers, users, observers and regulators are viewing critically not so much these products' true and real benefit to all concerned, but the risks involved in their implementation. The outcome remains to be seen, but we must expect changes. This could come in the form of more severe regulatory mandates or greater levels of obligatory disclosure, and whatever the outcome, it will determine the way in which derivatives survive and develop. Essentially the question is not so much about their continued presence but more to do with their health, status and dominance.

Derivatives have been getting a lot of media attention and, justifiably, the press has not always been complimentary. Is this a storm in a teacup or is something going fundamentally wrong?

In a number of instances now and with increasing frequency, there have been substantial financial defaults often associated with large monetary losses. Often derivatives have been accused of being the villain of the piece. One-off isolated instances, the protagonists of derivatives will argue, but even as a committed supporter of the use of derivatives I cannot agree. In terms of the size of the exposures, the degree of leverage and amounts of money involved in the defaults, these incidents are now too large and too common to write off as isolated instances. I have no doubt that the commodity markets will continue to be haunted by the names Procter & Gamble, Koshima Oil, Metallgesellschaft, Codelco and Atlantic Richfield, to name but a few, for quite a while. However, argues the gold market, these had nothing to do with our industry – it will be derivative business as usual as far as gold is concerned. I do not agree. Firstly, if we have seen derivative-induced defaults in other markets, we must assume that gold can just as easily fall victim to similar fiascoes. But, more importantly, if these defaults seen in other markets trigger the imposition of regulatory legislation, and it looks like they could in some form or other, then all the commodity markets subject to derivatives will under go far reaching and possibly irrevocable change. No commodity or financial market is an island neatly isolated from the fate of those markets around it and, for this very reason, this final chapter is devoted to derivatives in general and not only their presence in the gold market.

WHAT EXACTLY ARE MARKET PARTICIPANTS WORRIED ABOUT?

A number of worries have been publicly voiced and each market participant appears to have his or her own set of concerns. The users are genuinely worried about how the products are being marketed. Some complain that they are inundated, on a daily basis, by derivative creators with their hard sell marketing techniques, which do not give the end user a balanced view of the product. Disadvantages tend to be downplayed or not even mentioned until specific questions are asked. And even then, the end users feel that they may not have sufficient background or understanding of the products to know what questions are pertinent. Understandably, the end users then begin to question whether or not they are being marketed products that suit their needs or whether they are being directed towards those products which are either flavour of the month or have the greatest potential profit incentive for the creator. The derivative buyers, therefore, are experiencing a growing discomfort as they observe the way in which the derivative world is growing both in terms of complexity and number of products.

The regulators are worried about the proliferation of the derivatives business, which is essentially an off balance sheet phenomenon. Regulators will be more concerned about an industry that is virtually invisible (here I refer specifically to the OTC market), probably something that, through no fault of their own, they do not fully understand and a market sector that appears to be mushrooming in volume and growing out of control. Some estimates claim that the total notional value of currently outstanding derivatives is $4 trillion. Industry argues that the true value is substantially less since many contracts are either netted off or never exchanged. Proponents of this argument put the real value at $200 billion. While this is substantially less than the notional value, I find it cold comfort since it has been pointed out that this figure is of the same magnitude as the savings and loans crisis or the amount of loans associated with Latin American debt arrears[1]. Government officials have not forgotten the savings and loans crisis, the billions written off against Latin American debt or the collapse of the junk bond market. They genuinely fear a recurrence of some sort of wide-spread product- or sector-induced shock to the financial system.

They are concerned that management of companies involved in both derivative creation and consumption do not fully understand what their company treasurer is doing and the level of his market exposure. In some cases, management is not made aware of the level of these transactions until it is too late, but this is no excuse for loss of management control.

The regulators are also worried that a substantial proportion of the derivative exposure is held by a handful of large institutions and therefore the possibility of a default having a ripple effect through the first, second and third tier financial systems is greatly enhanced. The regulators feel that in protecting their markets, the derivative creators are a little sanguine about the possibility of the large exposures causing global financial stress. They argue that all is well until suddenly everything goes

---

[1] 'The Next Meltdown? Fears Grow that Derivatives Pose a Big Theat', *Barron's*, USA, p10, 6 July 1993

wrong, by which stage the stable door is wide open and the horse has bolted. Normal conditions do not alarm the regulators; rather they fear a sudden maverick incident, which statistically had very little chance of occurring, but may instantly move the goal posts.

In turn, the creators of derivatives are worried that the rush to regulate the markets will be disruptive and counterproductive. They are concerned that blanket regulatory constraints will exacerbate the possibility of substantial defaults and system stress by limiting liquidity at the very time when it is most needed. Since in recent years derivatives have in fact been the most profitable area of many banks' business, one must appreciate the creators' need to come to the defense of derivatives. As a bank's conventional business has shrunk, largely as a result of globalisation of markets and massive deregulation, derivatives provided an ideal opportunity for profitable expansion and development. Consequently, the creators have much to protect.

The derivative creators are also concerned about some of the motives behind the call for regulation, wondering if the issue is not just part of a much greater but hidden political agenda, for which we know many are famous on Capitol Hill in Washington, DC. Will the derivative debate be a trade-off for some other, but possibly unrelated, issue? In any case, will regulation imposed only in the United States, for example, have any beneficial impact in what is essentially a twenty-four hour global market? One can argue that regulation sanctioned in the United States will merely put local banks at an enormous competitive disadvantage and possibly force them to move their operating focus offshore. This does not augur well for a number of well established financial centres.

Accountants and auditors are concerned about a lack of disclosure, particularly as regards a company's exposure to the OTC market. Disclosure requirements have clearly lagged the rate of development of the derivative markets and the level of activity. Shareholders are also voicing this concern, claiming that these off-balance sheet activities can appear sometimes as an asset and sometimes as a liability. Consequently the standard set of annual accounts, published by a company, gives little in the way of insights into the real level of that company's market exposure. Shareholders are also concerned that companies are losing sight of the original reason for using derivatives in the first place. Many feel that trouble begins to brew when the motives behind treasury operations in a company blur and change from risk management to profit incentive. This situation is only worsened by a company offering to pay staff profit-related bonuses when in fact those staff should remain salaried and conservative risk managers. There is also a feeling that companies are using complex products which they do not fully understand or for purposes for which they were never intended in the first place.

Shareholders are now asking questions regarding the current level and sophistication of the internal checks and balances completed to assess derivative risk within a company. Is this sufficient? A perfectly competent stress test completed today may suffice but for today only. It is after all only a snap shot view of current risk and exposure. Tomorrow, external parameters may have changed sufficiently to render yesterday's stress test no longer relevant. There is also concern that whatever checks are done are not completed by an independent department, financially and emotionally removed from the treasurers. This can give rise to 'creative accounting' and a less than honest staff member can either paper over any cracks in an attempt to hide paper or real losses or give grossly exaggerated reports of financial gains and success. Could profit incentive schemes and bonus payouts calculated on shorter time horizons than the life of the derivative prompt and encourage this kind of behaviour?

Rating agencies are finding difficulties in assessing all this off-balance sheet exposure and the central banks, like the regulators, are saying that a chain reaction shock to the financial world cannot be ignored[2].

And everybody, to a greater or lesser degree, seems a little uncomfortable about the highly leveraged nature of the derivatives and the fact that they often, but especially under stress, do not behave linearly with movements in the underlying commodity.

What we are essentially dealing with here is a manifestation at various levels of the risks associated with derivatives. Six levels can be identified:

1 **Credit risk**: which lies in the possibility of a counterparty being unable to settle necessary payments associated with a derivative exposure. Unlike the exchange derivatives, which are cleared daily by the clearing house acting as a buffer between the buyer and seller, the OTC market is more subject to credit risk.

2 **Market risk**: the possibility of an existing derivative exposure being rendered loss-making as a result of the value of the underlying commodity moving against the derivative position. The element of

[2] Plender, J., 'Through a Market Darkly: Is the Fear that Derivatives are a Multi-bullion Accident Waiting to Happen Justified?', *Financial Times*, London, p17, 27 May 1994

risk is not only dependent on changes in the value of the underlying commodity but could be associated with equal validity to changes in other financial benchmarks such as interest rates.

3 **Liquidity risk**: the possibility of a counterparty, due to short-term cash shortfalls, being unable to settle payments associated with a derivative position. Liquidity risk can also describe the possibility of a participant being unable to exit from a market without substantial losses being incurred.

4 **Legal risk**: the possibility of a derivative contract being declared null and void.

5 **Operational risk**: the possibility of default as a result of staffing or systems failure within the corridors of a counterparty. In other words: the human factor.

6 **System risk**: this comes right at the top of the pyramid; the possibility of complete financial failure or meltdown within the international community as a result of the knock-on effect or chain reaction of one, but more likely a combination of, any of the other areas of risk.

The next inevitable step in the voicing of concerns is the open call for public investigations, recommendations and possible regulations. This is where issues become extremely emotive, but we have now reached that stage. Numerous official investigations have taken place, including those by the New York Federal Reserve, the Securities and Exchange Commission, the CTFC, the Bank of International Settlements, the Bank of England and the publication of the Group of 30 Report[3]. This latter report surprised me. I was expecting a substantially stronger conclusion, warning the world, if not about the dangers of the derivatives, then certainly about the leveraged nature and size of the market. Perhaps it was because the conclusions were neither strongly negative nor alarmist that it resulted in the media's attention being diverted away from what otherwise was an excellent piece of research.

The report that followed was very different and provided the media with substantially meatier copy and grounds for heated debate. I am referring to the General Accounting Office (GAO) report to the United States Congress which captured headlines by calling for urgent steps to tighten up the controls associated with all derivatives[4]. The report went even further and called not only for the regulation of the products

[3] *Derivatives: Practices and Principles*, Group of 30, Washington, 1993
[4] Waters, R. & Harverson, P., *Financial Times*, London, p1, 19 May 1994

themselves but for consistency in the regulation coming from the various financial authorities and watchdogs in the United States.

Interestingly, the major concern lay in the fact that the market was concentrated among a few large institutions and that these bodies could, via their derivative activities, undermine the stability of the underlying markets, causing a chain reaction of commodity price and associated company failures and ultimately a systems shock or even meltdown. As the *Financial Times* reported: 'at the end of 1992, a mere seven banks in the United States, controlled 90 percent of all the derivative activity in the country'[5]. Moreover, it was felt that these seven institutions controlled a good deal of the international trading. The sudden withdrawal of one or a combination of any of these banks could then give rise to severe liquidity problems in a number of markets and thus a chain reaction of failures could result.

The other major concern was that much of the growth in derivatives has been in the over-the-counter market which by nature is not subject to regulation and tends not to fall under the jurisdiction of any financial authority. In other words, the derivative market has outgrown its regulatory overseers.

The GAO report recommended that regulation could be instituted in one of two ways. The first would be to hand responsibility for the unregulated dealers over to the Securities and Exchange Commission. The other would involve splitting the responsibility between different regulatory bodies.

To begin to understand the issues surrounding regulation, one has to go back to the six risk factors and ask what went wrong with the derivative strategies that have been associated with the known defaults? One of the most publicised incidences was the failure of Metallgesellschaft's (MG) energy programme. Now I do not claim to understand fully the intricacies of what happened but I can try to fit the puzzle pieces together. In doing so, a fascinating picture begins to emerge. We know that in late 1991, MG began hedging energy derivatives. The oil market, at that stage, was in backwardation and hence MG's rationale of selling near term contracts and buying the furthest months out was completely in keeping with the market conditions at that time. These contracts were standard NYMEX futures but apparently, MG had embedded in this strategy a series of OTC options.

[5] Waters, R. *Financial Times*, London, p1, 19 May 1994

Having discussed this with a number of knowledgeable people in New York and Europe, I gather that the strategy of embedding the options complicated the overall strategy to such an extent that there were very few in the market who understood the programme and could assess the risk associated with it. This very large option exposure needed to be delta hedged and this may be where MG got into difficulties. The company became subject to risk in that market circumstances changed, rendering inappropriate MG's hedging strategy. A year later, by late 1992, oil reverted to a contango market and hence the forward price exceeded the spot price. This meant that MG was selling near by month contracts at a lower price than they were obliged to buy long dated contracts, hence they started incurring month-on-month losses. Market observers have offered a number of reasons why the backwardation disappeared and the contango was reestablished. Some have said that climatic conditions affected demand for oil products especially in North America. Others claim that Middle Eastern supply patterns also altered. A third group have suggested that while these overall supply/demand reasons are indeed valid, it is possible that the level of delta hedging associated with MG's embedded options was of a magnitude great enough to help turn the oil market from a backwardation into a contango. In other words, the hedging against MG's very own strategy, largely because of the volume involved, assisted in turning the oil market against the company. I am in no position to prove or refute this. But if this is indeed the situation, it is an astonishing case study and it goes a long way to confirm the importance to the market of delta hedging.

An article called 'Derivative Dingbats' in the *International Economist*, discussed the MG fiasco and in doing so, touched on the regulatory debate[6]. The authors were critical, not only of NYMEX, but also the CTFC, claiming that by insisting that MG met margin calls against their loss making positions, the exchange exacerbated the company's liquidity problems and succeeded in adding another nail to the hedging coffin. I take issue with this and in defense of the exchanges argue that MG, at the outset, must have understood that margin would be posted and in running an internal stress test, the company should have assessed, on a regular basis, the potential volume of the margin requirements. But, more importantly, this article seemed to miss the point about the level of

[6] Culp, C. L. and Hande, S. H., 'Derivative Dingbats', *International Economist*, July/August 1994

embedded options, which by nature were quite beyond the jurisdiction of the exchange or any regulatory body for that matter. It is no use blaming NYMEX, an exogenous body far removed from the source of the problem. NYMEX did its job within its mandate. The area in which the real problem emerged was one step removed from the exchange and its products. As I understand it, the MG problem was an over-the-counter issue.

I have no vested interest in putting MG under the spotlight. I have no doubt that the intricacies of any of the other defaults are just as fascinating and enlightening, each offering a sobering lesson. In doing so, however, I am merely attempting to demonstrate that these issues are substantially more complicated than they initially appear.

There is no denying it: we do seem to have a problem, perhaps many, and while I recognise and appreciate the concerns, I suspect that strait-jacketing the market with debilitating regulations will not necessarily provide the viable solution. Firstly, I do not believe that imposing regulations is going to succeed in stamping out either misuse of the products or the possibility of a systems failure as a result of the size or gearing of the market. In fact, there is an increased likelihood of regulations strangling and suppressing the beneficial side of the market while simultaneously failing completely to solve, or perhaps even address, the real problem areas. Secondly, as far as I understand the recommendations made by the General Accounting Office report, they are all sourced via government controlled regulatory bodies and not from the industry itself.

We must ask whether this is the right approach. Is there not a way of instilling a self-regulating code of practice from within the derivative market which requires a degree of sobriety and self control among the creators and the users of the OTC products? This essentially differentiates imposed regulation from heightened disclosure and mutual cooperation. In short, while I am all for a higher degree of reporting and more openness in the market, I am doubtful as to the wisdom of outright regulation.

To put the whole issue of regulation into perspective, we must bear in mind that while many of the concerns surrounding derivatives are unique, general concerns about systems, stress and possible meltdown existed long before the derivatives revolution. In this context derivatives epitomise financial history where regulators and governments continually struggle to keep up with a market, especially one that is evolving rapidly and has the bit between its teeth. As John Heimann, chairman of

Global Financial Investment at Merrill Lynch, observed: 'Traders are always ahead of management, management is always ahead of the regulators, the regulators are ahead of the auditors and the auditors are ahead of the lawyers'[7]. But how ironic! Is it not always the lawyers who make the most money when the whole thing ends in tears or when the music stops and one of the participants finds himself without a chair?

Having watched so closely the emergence of the derivatives, from unbridled market acceptance to genuine concerns being publicly raised, I must conclude that the process of evolution is still underway. Where will these products be in five or ten years time? I have no doubt that many will continue to enjoy a fruitful existence and will offer the creators and users respectively a means of earning a living and an indispensable vehicle to manage risk. There will be those who will use derivatives for purposes for which they were never intended. If so, we will continue to see derivative failures and financial defaults, perhaps of very considerable magnitude. But this is not the fault of the product and it is crucial that potential regulators of the derivatives understand this very clearly. Take away all derivative products and no doubt we will still see financial fiascoes, company fraud and misuse of management skills. The only difference will be that these maladies will manifest themselves in different ways and via other financial instruments perhaps quite unrelated to derivatives.

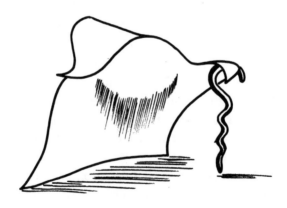

Mature Option

---

[7] Hiltzik, M. A., 'Derivatives: Perils of Ingenuity', *Los Angeles Times,* 12 May 1994

APPENDIX: THE FORWARD MARKET

PRODUCT NAME	DEFINITION	PRICE	US$ INTEREST	GOLD INTEREST (BORROWING COSTS)	MATURITY	PARTICULAR APPLICATION AND USAGE
1. Fixed Forward	Standard forward contrast locking in price, US$ interest rates and gold borrowing costs.	Spot	Fixed compounded annually	Fixed compounded annually	Fixed	Best used when the US$ interest rates are comparatively high and unlikely to rise further or could fall during the life of the contract. Best when gold borrowing costs are low and are unlikely to fall further or could rise during the life of the contract. Best used when delivery of physical metal is not of any concern.
2. Floating Gold Rate Forward	Standard forward contract locking in price and US$ interest rates. Gold borrowing is variable.	Spot	Fixed compounded annually	Floating calculated on maturity. Usually three month gold rate is used.	Fixed	Best used when the US$ interest rates are comparatively high and unlikely to rise further or could fall during the life of the contract. Also best when gold borrowing costs are high and could fall during the contract life. Best used when delivery of physical metal is not of any concern.
3. Floating Forward	Standard forward contract locking in price except both the US$ interest rates and the gold borrowing costs are variable.	Spot	Floating calculated on maturity. Renewal date flexible: usually done quarterly or biannually.	Floating calculated on maturity. Renewal date flexible: usually done quarterly or biannually.	Fixed	Best used when delivery of physical metal is not of any concern. Best used if US$ interest rates are likely to increase and gold borrowing costs are likely to fall during the life of the contract.
4. Spot Deferred	Forward contract locking in price but with variable US$ interest rates and gold borrowing costs.	Spot	Floating calculated on maturity. Renewal date flexible: usually done quarterly, biannually or annually. Some dealers report changes weekly.	Floating calculated on maturity. Renewal date flexible: usually done quarterly, biannually or annually. Some dealers report changes weekly.	Flexible with indefinite deferral on delivery subject to dealers' giving usually at least 45 days' notice. Notice is usually one full interest period.	Best used if the delivery of physical metal could prove to be a problem. Best used if US$ interest rates are likely to increase and gold borrowing costs are likely to fall during the life of the contract.

VANTAGES	DISADVANTAGES
ffers guaranteed & known contango throughout contract life.	1. Set delivery date.
lo active management after it is established.	2. Potential upside loss of 100% of contract volume if spot price at
Can be unwound before delivery.	maturity exceeds the contract price plus contango.
Possible to lock in US$ and gold borrowing to advantage.	3. Settlement payable only on maturity.
e applications)	4. Opportunity cost incurred if gold borrowing costs fall during the
	contract life.
	5. Opportunity cost incurred if US$ interest rates rise during the
	contract life.
	6. If the contract goes beyond 12 months, the dealer is quoting
	for a period beyond which gold borrowing costs can be hedged.
	This is reflected in the price quotation.
Offers guaranteed but only partly known contango throughout	1. Set delivery date.
contract life.	2. Potential upside loss of 100% of contract volume if spot price at
Minimal management after it is established.	maturity exceeds the contract price plus contango.
Can be unwound before delivery.	3. Settlement payable only on maturity.
Possible to lock in US$ interest rates. (See applications)	4. Opportunity cost incurred if US$ interest rates increase during
Floating gold borrowing costs can be used to advantage under	contract life.
tain circumstances. (See applications)	5. If the gold borrowing costs rise, the cash adjustment is payable
he 3 month gold rate tends to be cheaper than longer rates.	by the hedger.
e rates fall, the cash adjustment is payable to the hedger.	6. Final contango is only known at maturity.
the contract goes beyond 12 months, the dealer overcomes	
problem of hedging his gold borrowing costs (see Fixed	
wards) as the gold borrowing costs are quoted for periods	
rter than the contract life.	
Offers guaranteed but unknown contango throughout the	1. Set delivery date.
tract life.	2. Potential upside loss of 100% of contract volume of spot price at
Minimal management after it is established.	maturity exceeds the contract price plus final contango.
Can be unwound before delivery.	3. Settlement payable only on maturity.
Floating rates can be used to advantage under certain	4. Slightly more after-sale attention required if you elect renewal
cumstances. (See applications)	dates on US$ interest rates and gold borrowing costs.
	5. Final contango is only known at maturity.
Offers guaranteed but unknown contango throughout the	1. Settlement payable only on maturity.
tract life.	2. Slightly more after-sale attention required depending on selected
Minimal management after it is established.	renewal period.
Can be unwound before delivery.	3. Dealer can eventually request delivery but only after a reasonable
Floating rates can be used to advantage under certain	notice period. The dealer may call for delivery if eg the mine
cumstances. (See applications)	defaults on other contracts, exceeds credit facilities, operates at a
No fixed delivery date. Metal can be delivered on or before	substantial loss or the mine life runs out.
turity or deferred almost indefinitely.	4. The more regular the renewal period, the higher the cost of the
Can be unwound before delivery.	deferral and the shorter the delivery notice period.
Flexible delivery reduces upside loss potential. If spot	
ce > the contract price plus contango delivery is deferred	
dvantage is taken of the higher spot price.	

PRODUCT NAME	DEFINITION	PRICE	US$ INTEREST	GOLD INTEREST (BORROWING COSTS)	MATURITY	PARTICULAR APPLICATION AND USAGE
5. Partici-pating Forward	Forward contract locking in price but with a call option attached	Spot	Fixed compounded annually	Fixed compounded annually	Fixed	Best used if the potential loss of upside in the spot price is a major concern. Better suited to periods of high volatility. Best used when the US$ interest ra are comparatively high and are unlikely to rise further or could fall during the life of the contract. Also best when gold borrowing co are low and are unlikely to fall further or could rise during the life the contract. Best used when delivery of physic metal is not of any concern.
6. Advance Premium Forward	Forward contract with the contango partly payable in advance	Spot	Fixed compounded annually	Fixed compounded annually	Fixed	Best used in the early years of a m project when contango receipts ca coincide with cash flow requireme Best used for long term hedging ie 3–5 years out. Best used when the US$ interest ra are comparatively high and are unlikely to rise further or could fal during the life of the contract. Also best when gold borrowing co are low and are unlikely to fall further or could rise during the life of the contract. Best used when delivery of physic metal is not of any concern.
7. Short Term Averaging Forward	Forward contract locking in an average, not spot, price	Average pm/am London gold fixes over a pre-selected period eg one week to two months	Fixed	Fixed	Fixed	Best used when maximising reven from short-term production. Not a long dated product.

VANTAGES	DISADVANTAGES
ossible to lock in US$ and gold borrowing costs to antage. (See applications) Minimal management after it is established. Can be unwound before delivery. Upside loss potential reduced through the call option which is rcised if the spot price on maturity exceeds the option ke price. Most offer the facility to rewrite the contracts locking in her price during rallies. Advantage over options (min-max) in that the facility allows to lock in higher prices as the spot price rallies. The ndard min-max does not.	1. Settlement payable only on maturity. 2. Slightly more after-sale attention required if the option has to be exercised. 3. No contango is paid out since the contango is used to buy the call options. 4. The option is only exercisable if in-the-money. If the spot price exceeds contract price but the options are out-of-the-money, the option expires worthless and the premium (contango) is lost. 5. On using the rewrite facility, the upside participation is reduced. 6. Set delivery date. 7. Opportunity cost incurred if gold borrowing costs fall during the contract life as the option buying power is eroded. 8. Opportunity cost is incurred if US$ interest rates rise during the contract life as option buying power is eroded. 9. If the contract goes beyond 12 months, the dealer is quoting for a period beyond which gold borrowing costs can be hedged. This is built into the price quotation.
ossible to lock in US$ interest rates and gold borrowing ts to advantage. (See applications) Minimal management after it is established. Can be unwound before delivery. Contango is partly payable before delivery.	1. Set delivery date. 2. Potential upside loss of 100% of contract volume if spot price at maturity exceeds the contract price plus contango. 3. Slightly more after-sale attention required since early contango payments can be expected. 4. A premium is charged for upfront payment therefore contango earnings in later years decline. 5. Opportunity cost incurred if gold borrowing costs fall during the contract life. 6. Opportunity cost incurred if US$ interest rates rise during the contract life. 7. Beyond 12 months, a dealer is quoting for a period beyond which gold borrowing costs can be hedged. This is in the price quote.
Offers guaranteed & known contango throughout contract life. No active management after it is established. Can be unwound before delivery. Possible to lock in US$ interest rates and gold borrowing ts to advantage. (See applications) Reduces the probability of the contract price being the low for period. With the contango, the achieved price is guaranteed to exceed average of London fixes during the period.	1. Set delivery date. 2. Potential upside loss of 100% of contract volume of spot price at maturity exceeds the contract price plus contango. 3. Opportunity cost incurred in averaging rather than attempting to pick the highs. 4. Opportunity cost incurred if gold borrowing costs fall during the contract life. 5. Opportunity cost incurred if US$ interest rates rise during the contract life. 6. Beyond 12 months, a dealer is quoting for a period beyond which gold borrowing costs can be hedged. This is in the price quote.

GLOSSARY OF TERMS

ACCELERATED SUPPLY Gold reaching the market through lending and leasing before it is physically produced.

ADVANCED PREMIUM FORWARD Forward contract offering a constant **contango** throughout contract life; similar to **flat rate forward** and **stabilised contango**.

AMERICAN STYLE Options that can be exercised at any stage during its life, at or before expiration date. Contrast **European style.**

ASIAN OPTIONS History-dependent options where the outcome is reliant not only on whether or not the option is **in the money** at expiry but also depends on the average price of the **underlying** throughout the option life. They are used mostly (in the base metal markets) to reduce exposure or incentives to manipulate the underlying price at expiry. Asian options are also used by market participants who are obliged to have frequent exposure to the underlying asset over time. The options are then useful in capping the overall cost of the physical exposure and are ideal for producers.

ASSET-OR-NOTHING CALLS (PUTS) History-independent exotic options which have no income if the price of the **underlying** at expiry is below (above) the **strike price**. They are **in the money**, however, if the price of the underlying at expiration is above (below) the strike price.

AT-THE-MONEY OPTIONS Options with a strike price equal to that of the current price.

AVERAGE STRIKE OPTIONS Asian options where the income depends on an average strike price rather than an average underlying asset price.

BACKWARDATION A market situation where the spot price trades at a premium to the forward price. Opposite of **contango**.

BARRIER OPTIONS Unlike standard **European options** where the income depends only on the price of the underlying at expiration, barrier options are **history-dependent**. In other words, their outcome depends on the performance of the price of the **underlying** during the life of the option and whether that price breaches some predetermined barrier or level. See 'in' barrier and 'out' barrier options.

BINARY OPTIONS Unlike standard options which have a constant income, binary options have variable (usually all or nothing) pay backs depending on whether or not the price of the underlying meets some pre-agreed condition. Binary options can be either **history-dependent** or **history-independent**.

BIS Bank for International Settlements.

BONDS Means of raising debt through the capital markets. See also **gold-backed bonds**.

BREAK FORWARD OPTIONS Similar to standard **call options** except that they have no initial cost.

CALL OPTIONS Options giving the purchaser the right but not the obligation to buy gold at a predetermined (**strike**) price.

CASH-OR-NOTHING CALLS (PUTS) The simplest, **history-independent binary options** which have no pay out if the price of the **underlying** is below (above) the **strike price** at expiry. They yield a constant sum if the price of the underlying is above (below) the strike price.

CBOT The Chicago Board of Trade.

CCA Comex Clearing Association.

CFTC Commodity Futures Trading Commission, the futures and options watchdog.

CHOOSER OPTIONS Options bought and paid for but immediately after an agreed time, the buyer can elect whether the option is to be a **put** or **call** with an equal **strike price** and equal remaining time to expiry. The chosen put or call is a standard **European option**.

CIS Commonwealth of Independent States, formerly the Soviet Union.

COLLARS Options which have the same pay out as the standard **call**

expect that the upside is not unlimited. It is subject to a maximum. The option buyer forgoes any further income above this maximum.

COMEX The Commodity Exchange in New York.

COMPLEX CHOOSERS Similar to plain chooser options except that either the put/call **strike prices** or the put/call time to expiry (or both) are not equal.

COMPOUND OPTIONS These are options on options. The underlying asset is an option rather than a tangible commodity or security. Valuation of the option is complicated by the fact that two expiry dates must be accounted for: the time to expiration of the compound and the time to expiration of the underlying option.

CONTANGO A market situation where the spot price is lower than the forward quotation; the differential representing the carrying (financing) costs and prevailing interest rates. Opposite of **backwardation**.

COST CURVE Graphical representation of the costs of producing a metal for an entire primary industry. Usually cumulative output expressed in percent plotted against unit operating costs.

COUPON Annual interest rate associated with capital market bond issues.

DOWN-AND-IN CALLS A **barrier** option where the call is paid for up front but not received until the knock-in barrier is reached. See also **up-and-in calls**.

DOWN-AND-OUT CALLS A **barrier** option where the standard calls are paid for and exist until such time as the price of the underlying falls below a predetermined barrier after which the options cease to exist.

DOWN-AND-IN PUTS A **barrier** option where the put is paid for up front but not received until the knock-in barrier is reached. See also **up-and-in puts**.

DOWN-AND-OUT PUTS A **barrier** option where the standard puts are paid for and exist until such time as the price of the underlying falls below the predetermined barrier after which the options cease to exist.

EMCF European Monetary Co-operation Fund.

EUROPEAN STYLE An option that can only be exercised on the date of expiry.

EXCHANGE OPTIONS (1) Options offered by an exchange. They are a standard contract subject to the rules and regulations of the governing exchange. The COMEX option offers the buyer a COMEX futures contract should the option be exercised.

EXCHANGE OPTIONS (2) Exotic options which allow the holder to exchange one underlying asset for another.

EXERCISING AN OPTION The option purchaser holds the writer (seller) of an option to the agreed contract.

EXOTIC OPTIONS Generic term for the more sophisticated option strategy which has features over and above the basic contracts.

EXPLOSIVE OPTIONS See **knock-out options**.

FLAT RATE FORWARD Forward contract offering a constant **contango** throughout the life of the contract. Similar to **advanced premium forward** and **stabilised contango**.

GOFO Reuters screen code for the daily gold lease rates.

GOLD-BACKED BONDS Debt raised through the capital markets issued with a gold options alternative to enhance the value/attraction of the investment.

GOLD LOAN A means of raising capital for project financing which involves monetising gold.

HISTORY-DEPENDENT OPTIONS Options whose outcome at expiry is dependent on the price performance of the **underlying** throughout the life of the option. Sometimes also called path dependent. See also **history-independent options**.

HISTORY-INDEPENDENT OPTIONS Options whose outcome is based entirely on the price of the **underlying** at expiration date. The price performance of the underlying during the life of the option is irrelevant. Standard **European** and **American options** are history independent. Sometimes also called path independent. See also **history-dependent options**.

IFS International Financial Statistics.

IMF International Monetary Fund.

IMM International Monetary Market.

'IN' BARRIER OPTIONS Options which are paid for at the time of the initial transaction but are not received until a specified price level (the barrier or the knock-in boundary) is broken. If the barrier is broken at some stage during the option's life, then the buyer receives a standard **European** option with a **strike price** and time to expiration. If the barrier is not broken, then at expiry, the holder receives a cash rebate.

IN-THE-MONEY OPTIONS Options which have a positive **intrinsic value** are said to be in the money. In the case of a **call**, it is in the money when the **strike price** is lower than the current price. A **put** option is in the money when the strike price is higher than the current price.

INTRINSIC VALUE (of an option) The difference between the **strike price** and current price of the underlying commodity.

KNOCK-OUT OPTIONS Exotic options whereby the contract is cancelled if the spot price breaks through an agreed price. See **up-and-out puts** and **down-and-out calls**. The knock-out option is priced differently since it can explode or be cancelled while theoretically it still has **time value**.

Knock-out Option

LIMIT DOWN Arbitrary price level below which trading on a Futures and Option Exchange ceases during that trading day. Imposed to prevent very sharp price declines in futures prices and are adjusted from time to time at the discretion of the Exchange. See **limits**.

LIMITS Arbitrary price barriers imposed by Futures and Options Exchanges to limit severe price movements during a trading day. There are no limits in the spot market. See **limit up** and **limit down**.

LIMIT UP Arbitrary price level above which trading on a Futures and Option Exchange ceases during that trading day. Imposed to prevent very sharp price increases in futures prices and are adjusted from time to time at the discretion of the Exchange.

LIQUIDITY The volume of business or turnover on an exchange or any market forum; can be applied to either the paper market or the physical.

LOAN DRAW DOWN Mechanism by which gold used for financing is monetised usually with a sale of gold into the spot market or delivery against a forward contract.

LOCO Physical location of metal. Unless otherwise stated, price quotations imply delivery loco London.

LONG To be long of a commodity or associated futures or options contract is to have been a buyer. Contrast **short**.

LOOKBACK OPTIONS A **history-dependent** option where the income is reliant not only on whether the option is **in the money** at expiry, but also on the maximum or minimum price achieved by the **underlying** during at least some part of the option life.

MATURITY DATE Date on which an option matures; when it is either **exercised** or it expires worthless. Also known as expiration date.

MARGIN The cash deposit against a paper contract payable as a guarantee. An initial payment is usually made and thereafter further margin requirements may have to be met depending on the performance of the contract throughout its life.

MULTIPLE-OPTION FINANCING Term used in bullion financing in which the **gold loan** agreement is flexible in that the borrower can elect to make capital and interest payments in either gold or hard currency.

NAKED OPTIONS Options granted and left unhedged or exposed to potential **exercising**.

Naked Option

OPEN OUTCRY Method of trading any commodity where dealers face each other in a dealing ring or pit and there is direct communication. Contrast **screen trading.**

OUT-OF-THE-MONEY OPTIONS Options that have no **intrinsic value** are said to be out of the money. A **call** is out of the money when the **strike price** is higher than the current price. A **put** is when the strike price is lower than the current price.

OTC Over-the-counter; term used to describe an option that is written and traded through principals rather than a exchange.

'OUT' BARRIER OPTIONS Options which are paid for immediately and exist until, during the option life, a predetermined barrier is broken after which the options are rendered null and void – they cease to exist. If the barrier is not breached, the holder receives standard **European options.** If the barrier is broken and the options are extinguished, the holder is then paid a rebate.

PRINCIPAL-TO-PRINCIPAL Bullion transactions executed directly between the client and the market makers without being channelled through an exchange. Used primarily by market participants who have actual physical transactions to complete rather than the speculators. Speculative business tends to be channelled via the exchanges.

PREMIUM The cost which the buyer of an option pays to the writer or seller of the option; normally only a very small fraction of the value of the underlying commodity.

PUT OPTION Option giving the purchaser the right but not the obligation to sell gold at a particular **strike price.**

REUTERS International screen-base news agency widely used by all metal and foreign exchange market participants.

SCREEN TRADING Method of trading via computer screens and telephones in which there is no direct contact between dealers. Contrast **open outcry.**

SDR Special Drawing Right.

SHORT To be short of a commodity or associated futures or options contract is to have been a seller. Contrast **long.**

SPOT DEFERRED Hybrid forward contact offering floating interest rates and no fixed delivery. More flexible than a conventional forward but without the cost of an option.

SPOT MARKET The immediate market where delivery obligations usually occur no more that two days after the transaction.

STABILISED CONTANGO Forward contract offered by the South African Reserve Bank to the SA mines. See **flat rate forward** or **advance premium forward**.

STRIKE PRICE The agreed price at which the option can be exercised which will be equal to, higher or lower than the current price of the underlying.

SWAP A spot sale with a simultaneous equal forward purchase of equal tonnage. This is the definition of a gold or bullion swap which may differ from the term used by the foreign exchange markets.

SYNTHETIC GOLD LOAN A means of raising finance using the gold forward market which does not result in the monetising of physical metal.

TIME VALUE Option value associated with the time left to maturity, since during its life an option can move **in** and **out of the money**.

UNDERLYING Shortened term for the underlying commodity upon which futures and options are traded.

UP-AND-IN CALLS A **barrier option** where the call is paid for at the time of transaction but is not received until the predetermined knock-in barrier is reached. Differs from **down-and-in calls** in that the price of the **underlying** is initially below the barrier.

UP-AND-IN PUTS A **barrier option** where the put is paid for immediately but is not received until the predetermined knock-in barrier is reached. Differs from **down-and-in puts** in that the price of the **underlying** is initially below the barrier.

UP-AND-OUT CALLS A **barrier option** where the standard calls are paid for immediately and exist until such time as the price of the **underlying** rises above a predetermined barrier after which the options cease to exist.

UP-AND-OUT PUTS A **barrier option** where the standard options are paid for immediately and exist until such time as the price of the **underlying** rises above the predetermined barrier after which the options cease to exist.

VOLATILITY The rate of change in the price of the underlying commodity.

WARRANT Option attached usually to a bond issue designed to give the holder a highly leveraged exposure to the underlying commodity.

WRITING OPTIONS Selling someone else the right to buy or sell gold at a particular price.

10K REPORT Set of audited annual accounts published and issued to shareholders. Differs from an annual report only in detail.

BIBLIOGRAPHY

Brown, Michael, 'Central Banks and Gold', paper to the Annual Meeting of the Gold and Silver Institutes, Arizona, 1990

Cameron, D., Dent, B., Pearman, R., *Mining: Accounting for Gold Loans and Forward Sales*, Ernst & Young, Toronto, pp 1–8, 1989

Christian, Jeffrey, *Why Gold Loans Are Not Important To You And Me*, CPM Group Precious Metals Quarterly Report, Gold, New York, pp 19–25, 1989

Cox, I., Report for the World Gold Council, 1993

Culp, C. L., and Hanke, S. H., 'Derivative Dingbats', *The International Economist*, July/August 1994

Gold 1980, Consolidated Gold Fields Gold Survey, London, 1981

Gold 1981, Consolidated Gold Fields Gold Survey, London, 1982

Gold 1983, Consolidated Gold Fields Gold Survey, London, 1984

Gold 1984, Consolidated Gold Fields Gold Survey, London, 1985

Gold 1986, Consolidated Gold Fields Gold Survey, London, 1987

Gold 1988, Consolidated Gold Fields Gold Survey, London, 1989

Gold 1990, Gold Fields Mineral Services, London, 1991

Gold 1992, Gold Fields Mineral Services, London, 1993

Gold 1993, Gold Fields Mineral Services, London, 1994

Green, Timothy, *The New World of Gold*, revised edition, George Weidenfield & Nicolson Ltd, London, 1985

Green, Timothy, *The Prospect for Gold: View to the Year 2000*, Rosendale Press, London, 1987

Green, Timothy, *The Gold Companion: The A–Z of Mining, Marketing Trading and Technology*, Rosendale Press, London, 1991

Green, Timothy, *The World of Gold*, 25th anniversary revised edition, Rosendale Press, London, 1993

Group of 30, *Derivatives: Practices and Principles*, Washington, 1993

Hiltzik, M. A., 'Derivatives: Perils of Ingenuity', *Los Angeles Times*, p1, 12 May 1994

International Monetary Fund, *International Financial Statistics*, Yearbook, Washington, 1990

Jacks, Jessica, 'Opting Out for A While', *Nikkei Research Institute of Industry and Markets Gold Report*, Tokyo, May 1992

Jacks, Jessica, 'The Gold Loan Industry', *Financial Times*, London, 14 February 1990

Jacks, Jessica, 'Forwards, Spot Deferreds, Options and Gold Loans', *Nikkei Research Institute of Industry and Markets Gold Report*, Tokyo, June 1991

Jacks, Jessica, 'The Importance of Hedging and Gold Loans in Mining Finance', paper presented at the Financial Times World Gold Conference, Vienna, 24 June 1991

Jacks, Jessica, 'Forwards, Spot Deferreds, Options and Gold Loans – An Update', *Nikkei Research Institute of Industry and Markets Gold Report*, Tokyo, April 1992

Jacks, Jessica, 'When? How? and What? Rather Than Why?', *Nikkei Research Institute of Industry and Markets Gold Report*, Tokyo, January 1992

Jacks, Jessica, 'New Trends in Gold Financing', paper presented to the Australian Gold Conference, Perth, 31 March – 1 April 1992

Jacks, Jessica, 'Hedging Techniques Used By Mining Companies: Futures, Forwards, Options and Metal Loans', paper presented to the First Annual Conference of the Mineral Economics and Management Society, Washington, 20 March 1992

Jacks, Jessica, 'Why is the Pool of Liquidity Drying Up?', *Nikkei Research Institute of Industry and Markets Gold Report*, Tokyo, November 1992

Jacks, Jessica, 'The Erosion of the $350 Per Ounce Floor', *Nikkei Research Institute of Industry and Markets Gold Report*, Tokyo, March 1992

Jacks, Jessica, 'New Strategies in the Derivative Business', paper presented at the Financial Times Gold Conference, Istanbul, June 1993

Janeke, Paula, 'Gold: Looking to the Futures', *Financial Mail*, Johannesburg, pp 100–101, 27 July 1984

Laing, J. R., 'The Next Meltdown? Fears Grow that Derivatives Pose a Big Threat', *Barron's*, USA, p10, 6 July 1993

Laing, J. R., 'A Nasty Surprise: Derivatives Bite P&G But Who Will be Next?', *Barron's*, USA, p15, 18 April 1994

Newport, Don, 'Gold Loans: Recent Developments', paper to the Institute of Mining and Metallurgy Finance Conference, London, October 1989

Nicols, Jeffrey, 'MetalsFax', American Precious Metals Advisors Inc, USA, 4 January 1993

O'Connell, Rhona, *Annual Review of the World Gold Industry 1989*, Shearson Lehman Hutton Inc, London, 1989

O'Connell, Rhona, *Annual Review of the World Gold Industry 1988*, Shearson Lehman Hutton Inc, London, 1988

O'Dea, C. R., 'The Guarantee That Wasn't There', *Intermarket*, pp 38–45, Chicago, July 1985

Plender, J., 'Through a Market Darkly: Is the Fear that Derivatives are a Multi-billion Accident Waiting to Happen Justified?', *Financial Times*, London, p17, 27 May 1994

Todd, C. J., 'Gold Loans – A Growing Mine Finance Option', *Engineering and Mining Journal*, London, pp57-58, August 1989

Turner, David, 'Recent Developments in Bullion Financing', proceedings from the IPMI Annual Conference, Boston, 1988.

Waters, R., *Financial Times*, London, p4, 19 May 1994

Waters, R. & Harverson, P., *Financial Times*, London, p1, 19 May 1994